William Allen Whitworth

Worship in the Christian Church

Sermons Preached at All Saints, Margaret Street in 1898 and 1899

William Allen Whitworth

Worship in the Christian Church
Sermons Preached at All Saints, Margaret Street in 1898 and 1899

ISBN/EAN: 9783337005047

Printed in Europe, USA, Canada, Australia, Japan

Cover: Foto ©Lupo / pixelio.de

More available books at **www.hansebooks.com**

WORSHIP IN THE CHRISTIAN CHURCH.

Worship in the Christian Church

SERMONS PREACHED AT ALL SAINTS

MARGARET STREET

IN 1898 AND 1899

BY

WILLIAM ALLEN WHITWORTH

LONDON
SAMPSON LOW, MARSTON & COMPANY, LIMITED
St. Dunstan's House
FETTER LANE, FLEET STREET, E.C.
1899

CHISWICK PRESS:—CHARLES WHITTINGHAM AND CO.
TOOKS COURT, CHANCERY LANE, LONDON.

PREFACE.

ONLY six of these sermons (III. to VIII.) were delivered as a consecutive course. The others were preached at various times, and are only connected by their general subject.

Consequently there may be found in the volume certain repetitions of statement and even some repetitions of language. I have made no attempt to eliminate such repetitions; first, because those who heard the sermons will desire to read them, as far as may be, in their original form; and secondly, because I wish to avoid the pretension of putting forth anything like a digested treatise on Christian worship.

The sermons must be taken simply as an example of the way in which a busy parish priest calls his congregation to join him in studying a fundamental subject of religion, using materials ready to hand, and accessible to all.

I have tried to furnish my hearers with such references as should guard them against prevalent misconceptions about the teaching and practice of the Primitive Church, and should enable them to distinguish between that which is Mediæval, and that which is Catholic.

I have spoken throughout from the standpoint of an English Churchman who believes in the living entity and spiritual competence of his Church, and acknowledges without *arrière pensée* the authority of the incomparable Book of Common Prayer.

W. A. W.

ALL SAINTS' VICARAGE,
   MARGARET STREET, W.
     September 20*th*, 1899.

CONTENTS.

		PAGE
I.	THE FUNDAMENTAL RULE OF WORSHIP	1
	Note on the Distinction between the First and Second Commandments	18
II.	WORSHIP IN THE NAME OF CHRIST	22
	The Hymn to Christ — "Te Deum Laudamus"	40
III.	THE BREAKING OF BREAD AT JERUSALEM	43
IV.	THE BREAKING OF BREAD AT TROAS	59
	Hymn of Approach to the Altar	76
V.	THE EUCHARIST IN THE FIRST CENTURY	78
VI.	THE EUCHARIST IN THE SECOND CENTURY	94
VII.	THE EUCHARIST IN THE THIRD CENTURY	111
VIII.	THE EUCHARIST IN THE FOURTH CENTURY	125
IX.	THE DIVINE OFFICE	145
X.	THE LITURGY	162
	Note: Appreciation of the Book of Common Prayer	181
XI.	THE LORD'S DAY	192
XII.	THE DOCTRINE OF CHRISTIAN WORSHIP	212
	Note on the Mind of the Church of England as to "Hearing Mass"	231

WORSHIP IN THE CHRISTIAN CHURCH.

I.

THE FUNDAMENTAL RULE OF WORSHIP.

"Thou shalt not make unto thee any graven image, or any likeness of any thing that is in heaven above, or that is in the earth beneath, or that is in the water under the earth: thou shalt not bow down thyself to them, nor serve them."—*Exodus*, xx. 4, 5.

IF we are to worship aright, we must worship the right person, and we must worship Him in the right way.

If we do not worship the right person, we break the first commandment.

If we worship the right person but do not worship Him in the right way, we break the second commandment.

Both of these commandments, interpreted in the spirit rather than in the letter, are for all time;—nay more, we may venture to say that they are for eternity. For neither on earth now, nor in heaven hereafter, may we give to another the honour which belongs to God; neither on earth nor in heaven is the true God to be worshipped, save in the order of His own appointment. The first commandment bids us have none other gods; the second warns us that even though we worship the true God, we may not worship Him according to our own ideas, nor after the inventions of man.

The first commandment is the foundation of all religion: the second is the fundamental and eternal law of worship.

Worship is divided into two parts, (1) interior worship and (2) exterior worship.

Interior worship denotes the devotion of the heart; it is the submission of the will to the person or the object, right or wrong, which is allowed to direct and rule the life. Exterior worship is the use of prayer and sacraments and religious rites; it is made up of actions whereby we express faith and devotion and adoration, and profess that all that we are and all that we have are at the disposal of Him whom we name God.

Amongst those who have received a revelation of the true God,—certainly amongst those who profess and call themselves Christians,—it is hardly conceivable that the first commandment can be broken except by *interior worship*. When we say that a man worships money we speak of interior worship. We do not suppose that a god of gold is set up in his oratory or that he invokes in sacred rites the god of Good Fortune. But we mean that he allows the desire for wealth to have that power and influence in the direction of his life which ought to be allowed only to the law of God. His life is ruled not by the consideration of that which is right in the sight of God, but by a worldly prudence and foresight of which the motive is only the acquisition of material wealth. In similar language St Paul writes to the Philippians of some " whose god is their belly." The gratification of the bodily appetites had become the ruling passion of their life, justifying so startling a definition of their worship. But the very best amongst us have to be constantly on the watch against any overweening love of the world or the things of the world, lest these things should in fact become other gods, owning the allegiance of our hearts. The world and the flesh, pleasure, ease and self-indulgence, praise and power—all these compete for the throne within us: they are of the number of the "other gods" whom we are bound to renounce.

It is by interior worship that we make a false god: it needs no outward bowing of the knee, no sacramental observance, to place these rival powers on the throne that belongs to God. It only needs the consent of our heart and the surrender of our will to the unworthy object—and forthwith we have another god. Therefore the first commandment does not even name worship: the very foundation of idolatry is reached in the words, "Thou shalt *have* none other gods but me."

The second commandment, on the other hand, makes no reference to divers and strange gods. It treats of the mode in which the true God is to be approached in the solemnities of exterior worship. In that version of the second commandment with which we are most familiar, the word "worship" is used; and it is used in that popular sense in which it denotes not the attitude of the heart towards God, but the offering of the sacrifice of prayer and praise, of holy rite and sacrament. The commandment treats of exterior worship, whether in the privacy of the closet, or in the concurrence of united or family prayer, or in the public services of the Church. It lays down a fundamental rule of worship which in principle must be applicable to all times.

But if we are to apply the commandment rightly to our own circumstances we ought to study it first in reference to those to whom it was first delivered.

From the time of Abraham the chosen people had been separated by God, called out of the world, and enlightened by such revelations of his truth as had not been vouchsafed to others. They were in advance of their age in their knowledge of the one God; and though for a long time during their sojourn in Egypt He had made no sign on their behalf, they lived on the tradition of the promises and pledges of his presence which had been given to their fathers. But as time went on, the remembrance of past mercies grew weak, the brightness of tradition faded, and the verities enshrined in the name of the Lord were forgotten, until God revealed Himself anew to Moses in the bush, and made

Moses the mediator of a new deliverance for the people. Thus faith was revived amongst them. It is written that "the people believed: and when they heard that the Lord had visited the children of Israel, and that He had looked upon their affliction, then they bowed their heads and worshipped." But, I repeat, the revelation which they had received placed them altogether in advance of their age; and to live up to such a revelation was a matter of spiritual difficulty. Other nations had material or visible objects to which they could point and say, "*There is God.*" I am not referring now to those whose religion was a terror and their worship a service of devils, but to those who believed in beneficent gods, whom they could regard, if not with love, at least with respect. Invariably there was something within reach of their natural faculties to constitute a local presence, to spare them some spiritual strain in worship. They could look to the sun, the source of light, and say, "*There is God,*" or they could look to the river which fertilized the land, and say, "*There is God.*" They could see something more than human in the instinct or strength of the beast, or in the quaint habits of the bird, and they could say of either, "*There is God.*" There was always something at hand to make it possible to bring down the action of worship from the region of spiritual devotion, to the sphere of mechanical performance. The mind did not need to soar to Heaven, for the local god was at hand to be seen and touched. Even if the worshipper knew that the material thing was but the type or the exemplar of an unseen power behind, if at his best he could aspire to some sort of communion with the unseen, still the sluggish imagination could always find a refuge in the visible object, and so escape the necessity of spiritual effort.

But the God of the Hebrews belonged altogether to the spiritual world. He could not be localized : He could not be presented under any material form. Until a time subsequent to that which we are now considering He had no tabernacle, no holy place. There was nothing concerning which it could be said, " This is God," and unless the beacon of fire and cloud that led the way in the wilderness is to be regarded as a shekinah of his presence, there was no place concerning which it could be said that here rather than elsewhere, here is God.[1] Thus severely

---

[1] Even afterwards, when the Tabernacle was set up, though it was the symbol of God's dwelling among his

were the children of Israel being taught the lesson that "God is a spirit, and they that worship Him must worship Him in spirit and in truth."

But it was a hard lesson, because (as I have said) it was so much in advance of the times. They believed that Jehovah was in a special sense their own God. They acknowledged the deliverance from Egypt as his work. But where was He? Might they not give some material form to their worship? might they have something to point to, of which it might be said, "This be thy God, O Israel, which brought thee out of the land of Egypt." They had no desire to worship another god, but in the worship of Jehovah Himself might they not have some material help? something near them; something to gaze upon; something by which and through which they might worship the true God?

But no. The second commandment was proclaimed with all the thunderings of Sinai. "Thou shalt not make to thyself any graven

---

people, there was a significant avoidance of anything that should seem to localize God. The ark was essentially the *ark of the covenant*, and its contents were not symbols of a presence, but pledges of God's covenant with his people and memorials of special mercies.

image, nor the likeness of anything : thou shalt not bow down to them nor worship them."

That the commandment had the significance which I have ascribed to it—that it refers not to the worship of false gods but to the superstitious worship of the true God, is very clear when we study the events recorded in the thirty-second chapter. Moses was still in the Mount. He was gone a long time, and the people became impatient. Moses was the medium through whom they had received the revelation of God —and if Moses was lost it seemed almost as if God Himself were lost to them.

"So they gathered themselves together unto Aaron, and said unto him, ' Up! make us God which shall go before us. For as for this Moses which brought us up out of the land of Egypt, we know not what is become of him. Make us God!'"

I must pause for a moment to guard you against the false impression given by the rendering, "Make us gods." The fact is that the Hebrew word for God is always used in these books in the plural. The word is plural in the first chapter of Genesis, and it is used in precisely the same form here. If you render it here by an English plural, you may as well translate the first verse of the Bible, "Gods created the heaven and the earth."

The people cried to Aaron, "Up! make us God." And Aaron took their golden ornaments and melted them down into the form of a calf, and fashioned it with a graving tool, and they received it with acclamation, saying, "This is thy God, O Israel, which brought thee up out of the land of Egypt." The calf represented to them none other than the God who had delivered them in the past. This was strongly emphasized by Aaron, who proclaimed, "To-morrow shall be a feast to Jehovah."

It was still Jehovah whom they would worship —the very God of their fathers. Their sin was not in choosing another and a new god: they would worship the God of their fathers, but they would worship Him as other nations worshipped their gods—according to their own device and after their own inventions, not according to God's covenant and his promise, not in the way which He had appointed. Therein they violated the fundamental rule of worship—the eternal principle of the second commandment.

In one word, that which the second commandment condemns is superstition in worship. Superstition means that which is over and above what is authorized or appointed. In true religion we worship God as He has taught us to worship Him. In superstition we worship Him according to our own will in disregard of his appointment.

Sometimes, in great distress, under the sense of sin, or the fear of judgment, men will seek strange ways of reconciling themselves to God. The prophet Micah represents such an one as asking, "Wherewithal shall I come before the Lord, or bow myself before the high God? Shall I come with burnt-offerings, with calves of a year old? Will the Lord be pleased with thousands of rams or ten thousands of rivers of oil? Shall I give my firstborn for my transgression, the fruit of my body for the sin of my soul?" And the answer comes, "He hath shown thee, O man, what is good." Obedience is the rule of worship, even as it is the rule of holy living.

Therefore the devout Christian makes much of Christ's word in all his approaches to God. In his private prayer he is not merely fulfilling the promptings of his spiritual nature; he rejoices to think that he has Christ's word for what he does; that he should enter into his closet, and shut to the door, and pray to his Father which is in secret.

And when he joins in prayer with his brethren, he is not merely satisfying the desire for spiritual association, he is rejoicing in the charter of united worship in Christ's own promise, "where two or three are gathered together in my Name, there am I in the midst."

Above all, when he draws near to join in the Eucharistic oblation, and to receive the Blessed Sacrament, he knows that he is engaging in no action of man's device: it is the Lord's own service, who said: "*Do this; Take; Eat; Drink.*"

If our worship is to be offered for the glory of God, it must be offered according to God's will. Self-will can never glorify Him. And his will revealed to us becomes his law, his ordinance. The rule of worship is therefore the same for all time. We have always to ask, What hath God spoken? What hath Christ in his Church ordained?

Nevertheless, men are continually propounding their own ideas as to worship, in place of the rules which God's Holy Word enjoins.

One man says, " I will say my prayers at home,

or I will praise God in my heart as I study the wonders of science, or as I meditate upon the beauties of nature." But it is written that we forsake not the assembling of ourselves together, but that we speak to one another in psalms and hymns and spiritual songs. It is well that men should recognize God's hand in the wonders of science, and ascribe to Him the beauty of creation. This may constitute indeed a worthy act of interior worship, but it cannot dispense us from the obligation of exterior worship or from "the virtue of religion." In every dispensation of God's grace, religious duties have been imposed upon men, and in the services of religion they have found access to God, and have done homage to his divine sovereignty. Interior worship is, doubtless, the basis of that which is exterior; but to content ourselves with the interior disposition when the opportunities of exterior are appointed by divine ordinance in the Church, is to set up an imagination of our own against the word of God. This is, indeed, to break the second commandment.

It is sad to hear men speak of what they like and what they do not like, as though their own taste were to be the rule of worship. We have known persons leave one denomination of

Christians and join another, not from any consideration of the question which denomination fulfilled the more strictly the ordinance of Christ, but simply because the services of the latter were more to their taste than those of the former. They did not consider the responsibility of leaving that room in the Father's house in which his Providence had placed them: they did not inquire which body could show the clearest credentials of mission: they did not ask in which denomination was the pure word of God preached, and the sacraments duly administered according to Christ's appointment: they did not stay to ask what was right and what was wrong, but seeing a form of worship which pleased them better than their own, they incontinently changed their religion!

Perhaps no more signal violation of the second commandment could be cited than that which occurs when even good and religious people persuade themselves that they may worship God acceptably in other services, but that it is not necessary for them to receive the Blessed Sacrament. Of course if people are neglecting religion altogether, with all the rest they neglect their communion; and if they are not using the lower means of grace they are not fit to join in the highest act of worship. But amongst the less educated classes it used to be common to meet with those who apparently said their prayers and read their Bible, who were regular in their attendance at church, who were actuated by the true spirit of religion, who yet refrained from communion. They had perhaps received the Sacrament of the Body and Blood of Christ once after their confirmation, they hoped to receive it again upon their deathbed. But in the meantime they did not think it needful. If their conduct were prompted by a sense of unworthiness and by an exceeding reverence for the sacrament, one respected their sincerity, while bound to combat their scruple. If their neglect of communion were based on simple ignorance of Christ's institution, such ignorance gave ground for a lenient judgment, and had to be met by careful instruction. But, looking simply at the bare facts apart from their motives, here were people devoutly declaring that the other services were sufficient for them without that "which the Lord hath commanded to be received." It was substituting man's idea of worship for that which Christ commanded, and was, so far, the direct violation of the spirit of the second commandment.

And even amongst better-educated people, the tendency to substitute something else for that which Christ has ordained is not unknown. No Christian will say, in so many words, that if he be present at the Eucharist and join devoutly in the service, he is performing an action which may in some sense serve instead of the receiving of the Sacrament; and yet we meet with some who appear to think that if only they "hear Mass" every Sunday there is less need for frequent Communion. But Communion is that which Christ enjoined, and weekly communion is what the apostles taught and practised. Your non-communicating attendance may be a fitting act of devotion to Christ in that great mediatorial work which the Blessed Sacrament especially represents; but such attendance fails to fulfil the law of Christ, and if you let it serve as a plea for eating less often the Flesh of the Son of Man and drinking his Blood, you are displacing the ordinance of Christ by man's device: you are breaking the second commandment.

The virtue of religion is found in following God's commandment. Sacraments are efficacious, because Christ has instituted them; the bread and wine is that "which the Lord hath commanded to be received." But we are not to limit the sanction of Christ to those ordinances for which his own *ipsissima verba* of institution may be quoted from the gospels. He has other ways of revealing to us his will, and therefore of promulgating to us his commandment. "The Spirit of truth (he said) will guide you into all truth, for He shall receive of mine and shall show it unto you." Thus there may be rites and ceremonies for which the explicit warrant of God's word cannot be cited, which are nevertheless in harmony with Christ's intention and teaching, and are seen to be in accordance with the mind of Christ as that mind is revealed to the Church by the Holy Spirit. Where Christ has spoken and his word is recorded, that word is supreme. But there are many things in which He instructed his apostles concerning his kingdom which are not recorded. The great forty days between the Resurrection and the Ascension were especially devoted to such instruction, but we can only gather its substance and tenour from the subsequent action of the apostles. The laying on of hands in Confirmation is an example of a rite which we find the apostles practising, though no express command of Christ can be cited for it. It must have been one of the things in which they were instructed in the great forty days, or else they were led by the Holy Ghost to institute such a rite in fulfilment of the mind of Christ.

And when the apostles passed from earth, the Church remained "the pillar and ground of the Truth." Over and above the personal indwelling of the Holy Ghost in the individual member of Christ we believe that He is present with the whole body corporate, to teach us and to lead us into all truth. Therefore the voice of the Church is something more than the opinion of an aggregate number of individuals, and our immediate obedience to the Church is ultimate obedience to Christ.

We worship not in self-will, not according to the fancies and devices of men, but "after the due order,"—according to that which God hath spoken, which Christ hath ordained, which the Church hath delivered.

NOTE

ON THE DISTINCTION BETWEEN THE FIRST AND SECOND COMMANDMENTS.

THERE is much diversity in popular manuals in the application of these two Commandments.

The "Treasury of Devotion" proposes as questions on the First Commandment the following, which on the principles of this sermon would come under the second, as referring to unauthorized modes of approaching God: "Have I joined in any schismatical worship; separated myself from the Church; consulted fortune-tellers; used charms; given way to superstition?"

On the other hand, the "Priests' Prayer Book" declares that the Second Commandment "forbids us to put anything in the place of God." This is more commonly taken to be the very fundamental transgression of the First Commandment.

The Rev H. Newland in his Confirmation Lectures (1853) drew the distinction very clearly between having a God in our heart and rendering to God the tokens of reverence and worship. He practically applied the First Commandment to interior, and the Second to exterior, worship.

He is followed in the "Catechists' Manual" (1865) with the imprimatur of Bishop Wilberforce, where the subject of the First Commandment is explained as touching *whom we have as a God;* and it is laid down that as the First Commandment enjoins the worship of the heart, so the second enjoins the worship of the body. The application of the Second Commandment seems, however, to be unreasonably restricted to the attitude of kneeling, and other outward signs of bodily devotion, instead of being extended to include all that is embraced in the term "exterior worship."

The distinction is put very clearly by the Rev

Peter Young, who drank in much of the spirit of Mr Keble, whose assistant curate he had been. In his "Lessons on Confirmation" he says: "The First Commandment enjoins the entire devotion of the heart; the second insists on pure worship as the due expression of that devotion. If there is a tendency in men to forget God and give the heart to earthly things, so is there also a tendency either to neglect the worship of God or to worship Him in a wrong way."

The Rev A. W. Robinson in "The Church Catechism Explained" (1894) gives Polytheism and Idolatry as the key-words of the First and Second Commandments respectively. He, however, applies the First Commandment exclusively to the case in which "Imagination has darkened the heaven with gods and demigods," not including the case in which the powers of the world or the flesh possess the heart and rule the life. He rather makes room for this case under the Fourth Commandment, to which he assigns as a key-word *mammonism*.

The Roman Church, following St Augustine, counts the first and second as one Commandment. Yet Roman writers draw a strong distinction between the first part and the second part of the Commandment, practically making the same distinction as is made in this sermon. But in dealing with the first part they give prominence to the words, "I am the Lord thy God," which were altogether omitted from our Catechism in 1549, and though introduced in 1552, are printed not as part of the First Commandment, but (as also in Roman manuals) as a prelude to the whole decalogue.

The First Commandment ought to be regarded as co-extensive with the First Baptismal vow. The powers whom we are pledged to renounce are, in fact, aspirants to the throne of God within us, and are equivalent to the "other gods" of the Commandment.

The First Commandment thus reaches to the motive of our actions. If we steal we break the Eighth Commandment; but why do we steal? It is because we let some other power have the influence over us which God only ought to have, and in this we break the First Commandment.

The whole subject of worship in its exterior sense is thus left to the Second Commandment, and on the principle on which all the Commandments are applied, it must be taken not only to forbid unauthorized modes of worship, but to enjoin the positive duty of worship in accordance with the divine institution and ordinance.

II.

WORSHIP IN THE NAME OF CHRIST.

"Whatsoever ye shall ask the Father in my name He will give it you."—*St John*, xvi. 23.

THE distinguishing feature of worship in the Christian Church is, that it is offered to God in the Name of Jesus Christ. Before the Incarnation other forms of worship had been acceptable. The worship of the patriarchs was acceptable, though they knew not the Name of Jesus Christ. The faithful Jew performed rites of divine sanction, in which there was hidden a symbolic reference to the great Atonement. In sheer obedience, perhaps without intelligence, he may be said to have pleaded the sacrifice of Christ, and his worship was acceptable, though he knew not the Name or the Person of Christ.

But the position of the Christian is much more blessed. He knows, as the patriarch knew, and as the faithful Israelite knew, that God is One. But he knows also that there is one Mediator between God and man, the Man Christ

Jesus; and in the Person of that Mediator he enters into the presence of the Eternal. He offers acceptable worship in the Name of Jesus Christ.

In the passage before us Our Lord establishes the new and living way by which the faithful are to draw near to God in worship. "Hitherto" (He says) "ye have asked nothing in my name." Under the new charter the sacrifice is to be presented in the person of Christ, for the Church which offers it is the Body of Christ, and the sweet-smelling savour rises from his presence.

It is a canon of Divine Service written on almost the first page of our Bible, that worship can only be acceptable when the worshipper is acceptable. "The Lord had respect unto Abel and to his offering, but unto Cain and to his offering He had not respect." The offering and the offerer stand or fall together. God has no pleasure in the sacrifice in itself, whether it be prayer or praise, or costly gift. God's honour is found in the heart that presents it. To accept the gift is to accept the giver.

Thus it is written that "the sacrifice of a just man is acceptable, and the memorial thereof shall never be forgotten." Again, "the sacrifice of the wicked is an abomination to the Lord, but the prayer of the upright is his delight;" and, again, concerning the lawless man, "Even his prayer shall be abomination."

In accordance with this principle, our Lord gives his solemn warning to one who, without being in charity with his brother, would think to make an acceptable oblation to God:

If thou bring thy gift to the altar, and there rememberest that thy brother hath ought against thee; leave there thy gift before the altar, and go thy way; first be reconciled to thy brother, and then come and offer thy gift.

Any consideration of the conditions of acceptable worship will therefore immediately suggest a question as to the state of the acceptable worshipper. The man who is still in his sins cannot praise God. He cannot join with Holy Church in her high oblation. He can only say, "Wretched man that I am, who shall deliver me from the body of this death?" His only prayer is, "God be merciful to me a sinner." When he knows that he has passed from death unto life, then he will offer the sacrifice of acceptable worship to the honour and glory of God.

Thus we may put a spiritual interpretation upon Hezekiah's words:

The grave cannot praise thee: death cannot celebrate thee.

The living, the living, he shall praise thee as I do this day.

The Lord was ready to save me: therefore we will sing my songs all the days of our life in the house of the Lord.

Worship in the Christian Church has, therefore, a character of its own, because it is offered by Christ in the Church and by the Church in Christ; it has a particular worthiness of its own, because of the worthiness of Christ.

And if anyone thinks that I am making too much of an incidental phrase, interpreting as a new charter of Christian worship that which our Lord seems only to apply to the restricted case of petition, I appeal to the mind of the Church. For there is no point on which her teaching has been clearer, or her practice more consistent, from the first age to the present. The Church has never restricted our Lord's words to the mere granting of a petition. From the earliest times she has not only asked in the Name of Christ, but she has also offered in the Name of Christ.

Perhaps, in the present day, men of degenerate

faith think more of prayer than of praise; they think of what they shall obtain from God rather than of what they shall offer Him. But it was not always so. In the worship of the early Church, petition had only a subsidiary place, more prominence was given to the sacrifice of praise and thanksgiving, and to the glory of God.

And it is a singular fact that when we look into the literature of the first centuries and inquire how Christians then worshipped in the Name of Christ, we find the Name appealed to much more frequently in praise than in petition. The petition, "Grant this for the sake of Jesus Christ," is comparatively rare, but the ascription of praise, "through Jesus Christ," or "in the Name of Jesus Christ," is frequent enough.

Thus, in the Teaching of the Twelve Apostles, we have:

Thine is the glory and the power, through Jesus Christ, for ever.

In the Epistle of Clement:

Thou only strong to do these things . . . we glorify Thee through the high priest and surety of our souls Jesus Christ, through Whom be the glory and the majesty unto Thee for ever.

Worship in the Name of Christ.

In the Canons of Hippolytus a prayer for the newly baptized concludes as follows :

Grant to those to whom Thou hast already given remission of sins the pledge also of Thy kingdom, through our Lord Jesus Christ, through Whom to Thee with Himself and with the Holy Ghost be glory for ever and ever.

Again, in the Clementine Liturgy the most frequent conclusion of a prayer is the appeal to the Name of Christ :

by Whom in the Holy Ghost be honour and glory to Thee for ever.   Amen.

But it is needless to multiply instances. Whether in prayer or praise the Church always came to God in the Name of Jesus Christ, though the necessity of the sacred sanction of his Name was most strongly felt when the sacrificial aspect of worship was most prominent. And the sacrificial idea was always more prominent in the oblation of praise than in the preferring of petition. Yet we have our Lord's own word that we are to "ask" in his Name. *Every* approach to God is in fact to be made by the Christian in the Name of Christ. This has always been the characteristic of Christian worship, and every page of our own Prayer Book witnesses to the accepted usage.

We may, however, consider a little more fully what the statement means: We worship God " in the Name of Jesus Christ."

It means something more than the phrase " for the sake of Jesus Christ." It is something more than claiming the advocacy of Christ or pleading his favour on our behalf. It implies the truth of a great syllogism.

1. The value of any act of worship in God's sight depends upon several factors, one of which is the worthiness of the offerer.

2. In the worship of the Christian Church, Christ, who is possessed of all worthiness, is, in a certain sense, the offerer.

3. Therefore there is a great and exceeding value in Christian worship on account of the infinite merits of Christ.

The worshipper is represented as approaching the throne of God, speaking not in his own personality but in the person of Jesus Christ. It is as though he said, " I do not ask Thee to grant the petition for me, but to grant it for Jesus Christ. I do not ask Thee to accept the sacrifice of praise as if I were myself worthy to offer it. I ask Thee to receive it as coming from Him who is indeed worthy to offer. I speak in his name because I am incorporate in Him. I offer my sacrifice with his sacrifice, even with that which He offered on Calvary."

To speak or act in the name of another sometimes implies no more than a dramatic impersonation, as when our sponsors answer in our name at our baptism. Sometimes a person is legally authorized by a power of attorney to speak in the name of another. Under certain circumstances one may have a natural right to speak in the name of another, as perhaps a parent in the name of a child. Sometimes a person is entitled by delegation to speak in the name of a body which he represents. On other occasions we may be allowed to use another person's name in support of some request which we have to make; we are allowed to say that such a person of influence and judgment favours our cause.

But none of these instances seem to afford any adequate illustration of our title to come to the throne of God in the Name of Jesus Christ.

Our worship of God is offered in the Name of Christ, because we are ourselves in Christ, members of his mystical Body. "We dwell in Christ and Christ in us, we are one with Christ and Christ with us," not by a figure of speech, not by a forcible dramatic representation, but by a union which is mystical, sacramental, real.

There was nothing equivalent to this in the Old Testament. There could not be: for that membership in Christ, in virtue of which we draw near to God, is a fruit of the Incarnation.

In the Old Testament we read of prophets speaking in the name of the Lord, and of Levites ministering in the name of the Lord; we read of blessing in the name of the Lord, and sometimes of cursing in the name of the Lord. But in all these cases, that for which the sanction of the name of God is claimed is an action directed towards men. The prophet is the agent of God's operation towards man in blessing or in cursing: the motion is downwards, from heaven to earth. But in the worship of the Christian Church the motion is upwards, from earth to heaven; the action is directed towards God, in the Name of Christ. The nearest approach to such an action in the Old

Testament is found when the priest is ministering at the altar, offering sacrifice for himself and for the people. But in this case the priest is not usually said to be ministering in the Name of the Lord; the most that can be alleged is that the phrase, in Deuteronomy, sometimes includes this ministration as well as ministrations towards the people. But more strictly, when the service at the altar towards God is referred to, the priest is said to be ministering "before the Lord." From God to the people he ministers in the Name of the Lord: from the people to God he stands before the Lord to minister.

We may say, therefore, that there is no anticipation in the Old Testament of that which becomes the canon of worship in the New Testament, namely, that we worship God in the Name of Christ. The action of Christian worship is altogether unique.

Let me try to illustrate further the significance of our position.

See the man yonder who is worshipping God in the name of Jesus Christ. Who is he? The civil register of births will give his parentage. He may be the son of John and Mary Smith, born at such a date. But there is no birthright here that entitles him to stand before God in the name of Jesus Christ. We have to turn to another register—the register of a second birth. Holy Church took him in her arms and presented him to God in the laver of regeneration, that he might share the Sonship of the Only Begotten One. He was born again of water and of the Spirit, and that New Birth gave him the right and title to stand before God to worship in the Person of Christ. So we may paraphrase his prayer. He says:

"Lord, I appear before Thee to worship Thee —not as I am by nature, but as I am by grace. I stand in Thy presence not as the son of John and Mary, but as new-born in my baptism. I come before Thee in my Christian name, whereby I was incorporated into the Church, which is the mystical Body of Thine Eternal Son. O my God, through Thy grace I am no longer the mere child of Adam. Look upon me as Thine own child in Jesus Christ. Accept the sacrifice of praise which I offer not in my natural unworthiness, but in the worthiness of a member of Christ. For I dwell in Christ and Christ in me. I am one with Christ and Christ with me.

And in this union I make my oblation, I prefer my petition, I praise and glorify Thee."

To worship God in the Name of Jesus Christ is not, therefore, our natural right. The Name of Jesus Christ is not a phrase with which any-one and everyone has a right to endorse his prayers. It means too much for this. The title to approach God in this sacred Name implies a relationship to Christ which cannot be casually assumed and laid down at will. It implies that position into which we were introduced by the mystery of Holy Baptism, when, as the Catechism teaches us, we were made members of Christ and children of God in Him.

Although baptism puts us into the position in which we are entitled to offer our worship in the name of Christ, no one can suppose that the title thus conferred supersedes the necessity of personal and interior fitness on the part of the worshipper. But baptism is itself the pledge to us of grace sufficient for our sanctification. The Holy Ghost is given to us to convince us of sin, to move us to penitence, to guide us to the Cross, to assure us of pardon, to fortify us under temptation, to illuminate our path, to fill us with joy and peace in believing. In the power of the Holy Ghost we go from strength to strength, we experience the successive stages of the divine work within us, even as they are described in those thrilling words of St Paul: "Whom He did foreknow He also did predestinate to be conformed to the image of His Son. Moreover, whom He did predestinate them He also called, and whom He called them He also justified, and whom He justified them He also glorified." Therefore we are able to "draw near with a true heart in full assurance of faith, having our hearts sprinkled from an evil conscience, and our bodies washed with pure water."

But if our baptism constituted the union with Christ which entitles us and enables us to worship in his Name, we may well remember that the union which is first sacramentally established in holy baptism, is confirmed and strengthened and intensified, in Holy Communion: for (in the words of the Prayer Book), "then we eat the flesh of the Son of Man and drink His Blood; then we dwell in Christ and Christ in us; we are one with Christ and Christ with us." This brings us to a very important fact in regard to Christian worship. For if our worship is acceptable to God in virtue of our union with Christ, and if that union becomes most intense in our reception of the Sacrament, the conclusion logically follows that we worship God with the greatest acceptance when we receive our Communion.

I do not think that the logical connection is always perceived. It is a common occurrence to hear people speak of the highest act of worship and the sacramental feeding upon Christ, as though they were almost independent of one another. Some seem to think that we may at one time resort to the sacrament for the feeding of our souls, and at another time for the purpose of joining in the Eucharistic Service, and may make the latter to be the highest act of Christian worship. They do not perceive that it is the feeding of our souls that intensifies and raises the act of worship. Worship in the Holy Eucharist is our highest act of worship, simply because we are in the closest communion with Christ; and that closest communion is the fruit of our reception of the sacrament.

But another very important conclusion as to Christian worship follows here. We have seen that our title to approach God in the Name of

Christ is based upon our sacramental and personal union with Christ. But the mystical marriage and unity betwixt Christ and his Church constitutes a more perfect union, and a union less alloyed by sin, than the union of Christ with the individual member. The Church is directly the body of Christ. We are members of Christ indirectly through our membership in the body. His indwelling in the Church is something more than his indwelling in the several members of the Church. In whichever way we regard it we reach the same conclusion, that the Church is more worthy than the individual to offer to God acceptable worship in the Name of Christ. The Church, as the Israel of God, has more prevailing power with God than the individual.

Hence we perceive the value of the Church's prayers. They are more than the prayers of the individual: they are more than the prayers of the priest. When a righteous man prays for us his supplication may avail much in its working. But when the priest officially makes prayers and intercessions, these are not the prayers of a righteous man, but they are the prayers of the Church: their value is to be measured, not by the standard of the priest's personal worthiness, but by the title of the Church herself as the Body of Christ, to offer in the Name of Christ.

The priest, as the minister of the Church, may baptize, but it is the Church, not the priest, who presents us to be new-born unto God. The bishop lays his hands upon our heads in Confirmation, but it is the Church that invokes upon us the manifold gifts of the Holy Ghost. If the priest pronounces the benediction, it is the Church that pleads with God for the blessing. The Church prays in our espousals for grace of life. The Church calls down the Creator Spirit in our ordination. The Church visits us in sickness and commends us to God in death. The prayers of the Church avail more than the prayers of the righteous man, as the whole is greater than its part; nay, rather as the unbroken whole is often of more value than the aggregate of the parts into which it is divided.

People do not know what grace they are missing when they needlessly reject the prayers of the Church in favour of unauthorized devotions. Sometimes, while the Church is reciting her daily mattins, a worshipper will be occupied in private prayers, utterly heedless of the Divine Office. Of course, there may be special occasions in life in which one has deeply personal matters of engrossing interest to bring before God, and one seeks Him in his house, regardless of the circumstance whether the Church may be at the time calling the faithful to public worship or not. There are spiritual necessities which know no law. Those who are thus driven by the urgency of their personal needs to some private devotion which hinders them from joining in the public service will naturally choose the least prominent position in God's house in which to worship apart from the congregation. But these cases of urgency being excepted, we cannot but think that it is an action of the greater grace to join in the unity of the Body of Christ, to offer in the Name of Christ the appointed devotions of the day.

We have said that the offering of worship in the Name of Christ is an action performed in virtue of our own union with Christ. We associate ourselves with Him, He joins Himself with us in the offering that is made of prayer and praise to the Eternal Father. But while He is thus in a sense the offerer of the worship, He is at the same time One with the Father in the Blessed Trinity to whom the offering is made. The object of all worship is Father, Son, and

Holy Ghost, One God, and from this Godhead Christ in his Divinity cannot be excluded, even in a moment's thought. Just as, when speaking of the sacrifice of Calvary, we say that Christ was the priest who offered it and Christ was at the same time the victim offered in sacrifice, so we say concerning the worship which is offered in his Church that Christ is the offerer, and it is to Christ that it is offered. This double position of our Lord in regard to the ascription of praise is very remarkably indicated in the prayer which I have already quoted from the Canons of Hippolytus in the words:

Through our Lord Jesus Christ, through Whom to Thee *with Himself* and with the Holy Ghost be glory for ever and ever.

The Church has never let slip the truth that it is through Christ the one mediator between God and man, being Himself both God and man, that she has access to the Father, but at the same time she has never hesitated to make Christ Himself in his divine nature, the object of worship. Her normal form of prayer is to address God in the Name of Jesus Christ, but in worshipping God she is worshipping Christ. And if, instead of addressing God in the Name of

Christ, she now and again addresses herself directly to Christ, the latter form is pregnant with all that is expressed in the former. It is always God, Father, Son, and Holy Ghost, who is the object of worship, and it is always through Christ the mediator, God and man, and in his Name, that the offering of worship is made.

Through Christ we worship God: but the One God whom thus we worship is the Eternal Son with the Father and the Holy Ghost. This is the truth to which the Church witnesses every day in the great hymn to Christ, *Te Deum laudamus: Te Dominum confitemur.*

THE HYMN TO CHRIST.

1. Thee (Saviour Christ) we praise, when praise we God:
   Thee we confess, when we confess the Lord.

2. Thee the material Universe proclaims
   The father of Eternity to come.

3. To Thee all angels sing: to Thee the heavens
   And powers therein of every ghostly grade;
4. To Thee the cherubim and seraphim
   With ceaseless voice attune their song of praise:

5. *"Lord; Holy, Holy, Holy; God of hosts!*
6. *Thy Majesty divine with glory fills*
    The heavens above and all the earth beneath."

7. Thee the apostles' glorious choir extol ;
8. And Thee the tale of prophets laudable ;
9. And Thee the martyr-army, clothed in white.

10. Thee Holy Church confesses in her creed,
    As thus throughout the world she testifies :
11. *" The Father in his majesty immense ;*
12. *The Very Son, the Only Son revered ;*
13. *Also the Holy Ghost, the Paraclete."*

14. Thou King of Glory, Christ ; Thou only art
15. Eternally-begotten Son of God.

16. Thou tookest man upon Thee, man to save ;
    Nor didst abhor the lowly Virgin's womb.

17. The sting of death o'ercome, for faithful souls
    Thou madest entrance to the realms of heaven.

18. Thou in the glory of the Father hast
    Thy seat on God's right hand.   From thence
19. We look for Thee to come to be our judge.

20. We therefore pray Thee help Thy servitors
    Whom with Thy precious blood Thou didst redeem ;
21. Make them to be rewarded with Thy saints
    In endless glory.
22.   Lord, Thy people save :
23. And bless Thine heritage, and tend Thy flock
    And raise them even to eternity.

24. Thee day by day we bless, and praise Thy name
25. For ever and for ever.   O good Lord,
26. Vouchsafe to-day to keep us without sin.

27. Have mercy, Lord, have mercy upon us.
28. Yea, over us be Thy compassion poured,
    For we have set our hope on Thee, O Lord.

29. On Thee, O Lord; my hope is set on Thee:
    Confound me not unto Eternity.

III.

THE BREAKING OF BREAD AT JERUSALEM.

"They continued steadfastly in the apostles' teaching and fellowship, in the breaking of bread and the prayers."—*Acts*, ii. 42 (*Revised Version*).

IT may be profitable for us for a few Sunday mornings to trace the development of public worship in the Church from the beginning through the early centuries; first, to consider it as it is presented to us in the New Testament, and thence to pass to the witness of history, to the writings of the fathers, to the ancient liturgies; to study the mode in which successive generations have drawn near to God in united service in the Body of Jesus Christ.

Our subject is the corporate worship of the Church. And although we shall not overlook the offices in which the faithful speak to one another in psalms and hymns and spiritual songs (for thus they are gathered together in the name of Christ, and have the promise of his presence in the midst), yet our attention must be mainly directed to that solemn service instituted by our Lord Himself which constitutes the distinctive and characteristic action of worship in the Christian Church.

We intend to speak of the worship of the Church offered in the unity of the Body and in the unity of the Spirit: offered in virtue of the fact that the Holy Ghost is dwelling in the Church, and that the Church by his indwelling answers to her title as the Body of Christ.

We cannot, therefore, go back further than to the day of Pentecost. The disciples had been instructed as to Christian worship by our Lord in the days of his ministry, and notably on the night before He suffered. But they were warned that they must wait for the promise of the Father, tarrying in Jerusalem till they were endued with power from on high.

Not until the day of Pentecost were they consecrated as a Church and made to be the Body of Christ. Not until the day of Pentecost was it possible that the worship of which we speak could be offered.

Thus the passage before us carries us back to the true beginning of that action by which the Church approaches God in the covenant of Jesus

The Breaking of Bread at Jerusalem.

Christ. It describes conditions dating from the day on which the Holy Ghost descended in the likeness of fiery tongues upon the Apostles, incorporating them as a Spiritual Body, into the membership of which they were to admit others by baptism. That day about three thousand souls gladly received the word and were baptized. And then it is written that they continued in the apostles' doctrine and fellowship, and in the breaking of the bread and in the prayers.

This is, therefore, the very earliest record of the religious practice of the Church of Christ—the earliest possible record—for it describes what immediately followed the inauguration of the Church.

We are told first of all that they continued in the apostles' teaching. Doctrine and worship meet together: teaching and prayer embrace one another. There is no doctrine of the Church which is not to be traced in her prayers.

The apostles had much to teach. They had also much to learn that they might teach. We may assume that the Holy Ghost was daily calling to their remembrance the things that Christ had said unto them, and was showing them the full meaning and truth of his word.

We may assume also that they were daily searching the Scriptures of the Old Testament, and learning under the inspiration of the Holy Ghost how those Scriptures testified of Christ. In this chapter we find St Peter quoting David and Isaiah and Joel, and showing how their prophecies were fulfilled in Christ. In the next chapter he quotes Genesis and Deuteronomy, and in the fourth chapter two more psalms.

My Brethren, let us not depreciate the place of teaching in connection with worship. Let us recognize the wisdom of the Church in reading four lessons to us every day, in addition to the Epistle and Gospel. Let us try to learn even from the dullest of sermons. The Christian preacher possesses in these days no monopoly of doctrine: there will often be in his audience those who know more than himself, who can gather nothing new from his teaching. Yet if he bring forth out of the treasure house of God's word only the old things, there will be profit in hearing the old truths re-stated, the old promises recited, the old gospel again proclaimed. The chief obstacle to the ministry of preaching is found in hearers who are so confident of their own dogmatic position, that they cannot bear a truth expressed in any other terms than those in which it has become crystallized in their own minds. The preacher cannot please these, but he must try to help those who feel the need to be helped, and to teach those who desire to be taught, always setting forth the doctrine of the apostles, not only as the rule of Christian conduct, but also as the directory of Christian worship.

It cannot be supposed that the three thousand converts could be gathered into one building either for instruction or for prayer. The upper room may have accommodated the one hundred and twenty who were present at the election of Matthias, and it may be assumed that they were assembled in the same upper room, when the tongues of fire were seen to rest upon the apostles, and the rushing mighty sound filled the house. Multitudes were then attracted by the supernatural noise, and Peter probably addressed those who were gathered together in the open air around the house. Then we must think of many going and coming, inquiring of the several apostles concerning the gospel that was being preached, and professing themselves convinced; until by the end of the day three thousand had been enrolled. Doubtless the upper room would become a centre of the instruction which now they sought. But, besides this, the apostles seem to have made use of the opportunities afforded in the Temple, where some court or porch was at the disposal of any teacher who could gather an audience round him to hear the Old Testament Scriptures expounded. Our Lord Himself had used this liberty, as he explained to the high priest, "I ever taught in the Temple whither all the Jews resort: and in secret have I said nothing."

But they continued also in the apostles' "fellowship." It has been well observed that worship, whether true or false, implies a fellowship. St Paul assumes the same truth when he contrasts the table of the Lord with the idolatrous table of demons, and writes: "I would not have you to have fellowship with demons."

We ought to note that fellowship with the apostles meant fellowship, not with them alone but with God, with whom the apostles were in fellowship. St John puts this explicitly. He writes, "that ye may have fellowship with us, and truly our fellowship is with God and with his Son Jesus Christ." So the term fellowship has a very wide range of application. It denotes the Communion of the Holy Ghost, and it includes the common care for the weakest members of a body. The same word, κοινωνία, is used by St Paul when he speaks of the Communion of the Body of Christ, and the Communion of the Blood of Christ, and he uses it again several times when he speaks of a collection for the poor. It is glorified to denote that which we call κατ' ἐξοχήν, the Holy Communion, whilst at the same time the special circumstance of the Church at Jerusalem gave it a particular application at the period now under consideration; for in the passage before us, the statement of verse 44, "they had all things common" (κοινά), undoubtedly indicates one of the manifestations of the κοινωνία or fellowship of verse 42.

We have reference in St Paul's epistles to the poverty which prevailed among the Christians at Jerusalem. From the beginning there were many among them who had to depend for their daily bread upon the contributions which some of the richer members of the Church had the means of making. The apostles themselves had apparently no means of livelihood, and while they devoted themselves to spiritual offices, they had to depend, like the poorest of their flock, on

E

that daily ministration of a common table to which reference is made in the sixth chapter.

But the idea of Christian fellowship included all this, so that in the very early days of which we are speaking, the common meal, subsequently spoken of as the love feast, was as real a part of the religion of the Church as the sacramental breaking of the bread of which we shall speak immediately.

It has been said that the way in which "they sold their possessions and goods and parted them to all according as any man had need," would have been reckless, had they not looked for a speedy return of Christ. Even as it was, the system speedily gave rise to difficulties. The Grecian Jews thought that their widows were overlooked in the daily ministration. The apostles found that embarrassments arose from the confusion of spiritual and temporal interests. They determined to leave the serving of the tables to others, whilst they devoted themselves to the prayers and to the preaching of the word. We do not find that the system was tried in other churches, though the common table—the Church feast—commonly called the Agapé or love feast—was continued for a considerable time, and was held in close connection with the

Eucharist. It was established as a token of brotherly love and fellowship, and was, therefore, the more readily associated with the sacramental act of fellowship. The early Christians naturally followed the order of the Last Supper, when our Lord first joined in the social meal with his disciples, and after supper instituted the Blessed Sacrament. So it seems that the love feast was first held, and at its conclusion there came the Sacramental Breaking of the Bread. But so close was the association of the Agapé with the Eucharist, that it is sometimes difficult to determine which is being referred to. St Paul apparently refers to both together in that passage in which he condemns the abuses which prevailed at Corinth:

When ye come together therefore into one place, this is not to eat the Lord's supper. For in eating every one taketh before other his own supper: and one is hungry, and another is drunken. What? have ye not houses to eat and drink in? or despise ye the church of God, and shame them that have not? What shall I say to you? Shall I praise you in this? I praise you not.

Then he goes on to recite the institution of the Sacrament, and gives the warning about eating and drinking unworthily, and concludes thus:

Wherefore, my brethren, when ye come together to eat, tarry one for another. And if any man hunger, let him eat at home; that ye come not together unto condemnation.

Further, they continued in the breaking of the bread and in the prayers. I cannot doubt that the breaking of the bread in this verse denotes the celebration of the Eucharist, though there is ground to question whether the phrase, breaking bread, in the 46th verse, may not refer rather to the Agapé, especially as it is joined to the statement that they took their food with gladness and singleness of heart, the last words seeming to apply to the satisfaction of bodily needs rather than to the Sacramental act of Communion. But in fact at this time the two were (as I have said) closely bound together.

If we would picture to ourselves the Christian worship of these primitive days, we must bear in mind that there were no church buildings. We have not yet reached the time when Christianity became a proscribed religion, and the faithful were compelled to worship in dens and caves of the earth, but at the period with which we are concerned there had been no time or opportunity to provide any place of worship, except (it may be) that upper room to which reference has been made. Its accommodation must, however, have been quite inadequate for a church of three thousand members. Obviously the greater part of the Church's functions must have been performed at home, and we may think of the twelve apostles, each perhaps with the care of some two hundred and fifty converts, sometimes teaching a group in the temple, sometimes passing from house to house, presiding over the common meal and breaking the Sacramental Bread. We have, for instance, an example, in the twelfth chapter, of the Church in a private house. Peter was cast into prison, but it is written, "Prayer was made without ceasing of the Church to God for him." It was the prayer of the Church, but where was it offered? In the house of a good woman—Mary, the mother of John Mark. Thus we may read the details of the 44th and 46th verses of this second chapter as the natural explanation of the fundamental statement in the text. First we have the undoubtedly fundamental principles of church life defined—"they continued steadfastly in the apostles' doctrines and fellowship, and in the breaking of the bread and of the prayers," and then we have what seems, at first sight, to be rather a repetition, but is found to be full of explanatory details:

And all that believed were together, and had all things common; and sold their possessions and goods, and parted them to all men, as every man had need. And they, continuing daily with one accord in the temple, and breaking bread from house to house, did eat their meat with gladness and singleness of heart, praising God, and having favour with all the people.

The statement that they continued in the Breaking of Bread and in the Prayers, may be taken to indicate that there were other prayers than those which accompanied the breaking of the bread. The reference may possibly be to the prayers in the Temple, to which Peter and John are immediately found going up. But the close connexion with the Breaking of the Bread rather indicates some distinctive action of the Church. It would be an anachronism to say that they recited the Divine Office, and yet remembering that they were still devout Jews, we can scarcely doubt that the saying or singing of psalms would form a prominent part of their devotion, especially as we find the apostles continually quoting the psalms and insisting on their prophetic reference to Christ. And the Divine Office, as the Church has said it for centuries, as we say it still in mattins and evensong, is in its central feature the recital of the Psalter, the Psalms constituting the string on which are strung the pearls of collects, creed, and lessons. Perhaps, therefore, it is not too much to say that the present services of the Church, the Divine Office as well as the Divine Liturgy are both to be found in germ in the earliest worship of the Church.

The picture which we have been studying of the earliest worship of the Church shows the futility of the assumption sometimes made, that there should be no such thing as development in the services of the Church—that worship ought to be governed in this nineteenth century by the rules to which it was subject in the first.

The conditions and environment of the Church are always changing, and the Church, as a living body, must be in correspondence with its environment. The *principles* of Christian worship do not change—the notes of a true Church are to-day what they were one thousand eight hundred years ago. We still continue steadfast, as I trust, in the apostles' doctrine and in fellowship, in the breaking of the bread, and in the prayers; but it would be absurd to say that, because the Church in scriptural times possessed no buildings, and had no permanent altar, the noble sanctuaries of the present day are to be condemned as departures from primitive simplicity. There is no force in the argument that because the apostles did not use incense when they broke the bread from house to house, the Church was wrong in introducing its use in the fourth century. We might as well argue that because the apostles did not use electric light, our churches ought not to be lighted by electricity to-day. It is true in the Church as in any other living institution that

> The old order changeth giving place to new,
> And God fulfils Himself in many ways.

Yet there are the eternal verities which change not. Your worship to-day must be identical with that of apostolic days, not only in its general principles, but in all those conditions which divine authority imposes. It is true now as when the apostle first wrote it that the bread which we break is the communion of the body of Christ, and the cup which we bless is the communion of his blood; that as often as men eat this bread and drink this cup they do show the

Lord's death till He come. It is true now as when it was first proclaimed that there is none other name under Heaven given among men whereby we must be saved, but only the name of the Lord Jesus Christ—the Son of God who loved us and gave Himself for us.

Jesus Christ is the same yesterday, to-day, and for ever.

There may be new developments of the Church's worship. The ritual of an age when many worshippers can read, may differ much from the order of service when there were no books. As the centuries roll on the Church may adopt new modes of giving expression to the reverence and devotion of those who draw near, but there can be no new way of access to God. The accessories of worship may be multiplied, beautified, glorified: but there is no acceptable worship differing in its essential character from that which was known to St Peter and St John.

The new and living way which Christ consecrated for us through the veil, that is to say, his flesh, can never become obsolete. The great priest over the house of God exercises an unchanging priesthood: therefore we draw near, as the apostles did, as the saints of every age have done, in the old way which is still new, ever presenting and pleading the one full, perfect, and sufficient sacrifice, oblation, and satisfaction, which Christ made upon the Cross of Calvary for the sins of the whole world.

IV.

THE BREAKING OF BREAD AT TROAS.

"And upon the first day of the week, when the disciples came together to break bread, Paul preached unto them, ready to depart on the morrow; and continued his speech until midnight."—*Acts*, xx. 7.

LAST Sunday our subject was the breaking of bread at Jerusalem. We tried to picture to ourselves the worship of the Church in the very early days immediately after the giving of the Holy Ghost at Pentecost. We saw that the apostles had three thousand souls at once to minister to, and though some may have left Jerusalem soon after the feast, we have to set against this the fact that the Lord was daily adding to the Church those who were being saved. We saw the apostles busy preaching and teaching, breaking the bread and leading the prayers. The upper room in which the apostles were gathered together on the day of Pentecost doubtless continued to be a centre of teaching and worship: they also availed themselves of the facilities which the Temple afforded, and in some court or portico they might be found teaching all who were willing to hear. "Daily in the Temple and in every house they ceased not to teach and preach Jesus Christ." They used the Temple also for prayers: and when we read of Peter and John going up "at the hour of prayer, being the ninth hour," we understand that the purpose of these two apostles was to join as devout Jews in the prayers which were then being offered, though they would also use the opportunity, which the concourse at that hour afforded, of making known the glad tidings of the Resurrection. But they had no place where three thousand converts could come together for the celebration of the Holy Eucharist. The apostles could only celebrate for small groups of them gathered in different houses in rotation. So we read of their breaking bread daily from house to house, or house by house.

Before I pass on, it may be well to point out that this daily breaking of the bread, house by house, scarcely warrants the statement that the Christians in Jerusalem had a daily celebration in the ordinary acceptation of the term. If the three thousand were to receive the Holy Sacrament every week, no doubt the apostles would be celebrating somewhere every day—in certain houses to-day and in other houses to-morrow—but we cannot assert that there was anything corresponding to what is commonly understood by a daily celebration,—that is, a celebration of the Holy Eucharist day by day for the same congregation in the same place. No argument, however, against a daily celebration can be drawn from the inchoate practice of a time when the Christians did not yet possess a church building or a fixed altar.

Our subject to-day is the Breaking of Bread at Troas. Twenty-five years have elapsed since the first breaking of bread at Jerusalem, and the customs of the Church have become much more fixed. The first day of the week is now recognized as the special day of Christian worship, and on that day, as a matter of course, Christian people come together to celebrate the Eucharist. But the scene is no longer laid in the Holy City. We are carried to the shores of the Ægean Sea, to a city of Asia Minor, in which the Christians are apparently not too many to worship in one place. They have a meeting room on the third floor of a large house, reached, as is usual in the

East, by an outside staircase. We no longer read of the breaking of the bread from house to house; it was their settled custom to assemble in their upper room on the first day of the week. It appears from the narrative before us that they met late in the day. This was, perhaps, necessitated by the fact that they had their daily work to do. Sunday was not yet a general day of rest, and if they kept Sabbath (as those of Jewish origin probably did) they kept it on Saturday. They had a precedent for the evening hour, not only in our Lord's institution of the Blessed Sacrament after supper, but also in his first appearance to his assembled Church on the evening of the Resurrection Day. We shall find, however, if we continue our historical investigation, that in the next century an early hour in the morning was substituted for the evening hour, perhaps with the intention of checking such disorders as those which St Paul condemns in his First Epistle to the Corinthians, when he complains that either in the Agapé or in the Eucharist which was joined with it, "one is hungry and another is drunken."

That First Epistle to the Corinthians was probably written a very short time previous to

The Breaking of Bread at Troas.

the event which we are now considering. It is remarkable for its repeated reference to Holy Communion, and the more remarkable because it it is the only one of the epistles in which the Sacrament is directly mentioned. In the fifth chapter we have a probable allusion to the Sacrament in the passage:

Christ our Passover is sacrificed for us. Therefore let us keep the feast not with the old leaven, neither with the leaven of malice and wickedness, but with the unleavened bread of sincerity and truth.

In the tenth chapter we have direct reference to the Sacrament:

The cup of blessing which we bless is it not the communion of the blood of Christ? The bread which we break is it not the communion of the body of Christ?
For we being many are one bread, and one body: for we all are partakers of that one bread.

In the eleventh chapter we have St Paul's account of the Institution of the Blessed Sacrament, concluding with the important verse:

As often as ye eat this bread, and drink this cup, ye do show the Lord's death till he come.

Let me say a word in passing about this verse. It is not quite clear whether the apostle is still citing Christ's own words, or whether he is merely adding his own comment on the subject. There is much to be said for the former hypothesis: and the fact that in this view He speaks of Himself in the third person as "the Lord" does not necessarily condemn it. For He certainly speaks of Himself in the third person in the conversation with Nicodemus and on some other occasions. And though most modern commentators take the words as St Paul's, nearly all the ancient liturgies[1] quote them as Christ's own words, often transposing them into the first person, "As often as ye eat this bread and drink this cup ye shall show *my* death till I come."

I may remind you that in the Hymn of Approach to the altar which we sing here every Saturday night, the saying is implicitly ascribed to Our Lord in the lines:

[1] Dr. Neale and Dr. Littledale published, many years ago, a collection of the "Formulæ of Institution" from eighty-two liturgies. In about fifty of them the words recorded by St Paul are quoted (with more or less adaptation) as uttered by Our Lord. In many instances the quotation is literal with the simple change of person in the last clause: "My death, till I come." In a few cases only the words "till I come" are added at the end of the

Till He come fulfil his word,
Show the death of Christ the Lord.

But we have not yet exhausted the references to the Holy Eucharist in the First Epistle to the Corinthians. A little lower, in the eleventh chapter, we have the warning:

Let a man examine himself, and so let him eat of that bread and drink of that cup;

with the condemnation of those who eat and drink unworthily, "not discerning the Lord's Body."

It is the same St Paul who had so lately form given in the gospels. In other instances the saying is amplified, but the reference remains unobscured. For example:

(*Ethiopic Liturgy of St Basil.*)—"Whenever ye eat this bread and drink this cup, set forth my death and confess my resurrection, and make commemoration of me until I come."

(*Ethiopic of St Athanasius.*)—"As often as ye eat this Bread and drink this Cup, set forth my death and resurrection, and confess my ascension and my coming again with glory whilst ye wait."

It is remarkable that nearly every Liturgy that quotes or adapts the passage introduces the reference to the Resurrection, but the references to the Ascension and the Second Advent are more rare.

written all these earnest words about the Sacrament, whom we now see at Troas conducting the worship of the Church and breaking the bread.

But before we finally close the first Epistle to the Corinthians, we may note that it contains a reference to the first day of the week which illustrates the passage before us. This reference is found in Chapter xvi., verse 2, the verse which is constantly quoted in support of the weekly offertory:

Upon the first day of the week let every one of you lay by him in store, as God hath prospered him, that there may be no gatherings when I come.

The observance of Sunday as the day of worship has always been based upon the circumstance that our Lord first appeared to his Church on the evening of the Resurrection day, and again eight days after, that is, on the following Sunday. But apart from the inferences drawn from these two occasions, the earliest recognition of the keeping of Sunday is afforded by St Paul's injunction for the weekly offering, and by the account before us of the Breaking of the Bread at Troas. Indeed, beyond this, there is no further reference to the practice, except it be in St John's mention in the Apocalypse of " the Lord's Day."

We gather from the narrative before us something of the procedure customary at the meeting of the early Church on the first day of the week. The meeting began with instruction and discourse, teaching and preaching : it concluded with the solemn Breaking of the Bread, the Eucharist. The Agapé may have been held at an earlier part of the meeting. But it is more probable that the Agapé and the Eucharist were one feast. In either case the Breaking of the Bread, while it came at the end, was the great action in which all else culminated : it was so distinctly the prominent object of the meeting that it alone defined the purpose for which they came together. It is not said that they came together to be taught or to hear Paul preach. But they came together to break bread.

Some have curiously suggested that the Breaking of the Bread was put off until after midnight, in order that the faithful might receive fasting. The suggestion involves a most grotesque anachronism. The practice of preparing for baptism or communion by fasting is very old indeed, perhaps as old as the apostolic age,[1] but the rule of dating a fast from midnight was not heard of for twelve hundred years afterwards. Moreover, the narrative seems to imply that the Breaking of the Bread was thrown so late in consequence of the length of the apostle's sermon. If we were to suppose it to have been the custom for the faithful to assemble on Sunday evening to break bread, but to defer the actual Eucharist till after midnight, we should be establishing the practice of a weekly celebration not on the Lord's Day, but on Monday.

We must now face a fact which has startled many devout students of the New Testament; namely, the paucity and scantiness of the references in the sacred books to the central act of Christian worship. In the Gospel according to St John, we have a discourse of our Lord concerning the eating of his flesh and the drinking of his blood, but no mention of the Blessed Sacrament itself. The other three evangelists

---

[1] The fast before baptism is of much greater antiquity than the fast before communion. This is probably the reason why the Church of England in the Book of Common Prayer enjoins the fast before (adult) baptism, but does not enjoin it before the reception of the Holy Eucharist.

The Breaking of Bread at Troas.

record the institution of the Sacrament. But after that the sacramental Breaking of the Bread is only mentioned twice in the Acts of the Apostles, once as having taken place at Jerusalem, and once at Troas; and only in one of the Epistles is there any direct mention of the subject, unless, indeed, we include the implicit reference in the Epistle to the Hebrews in the passage :

We have an altar, whereof they have no right to eat which serve the tabernacle.

How are we to explain the fact that the New Testament says so little on so great a subject?

I. As the Blessed Sacrament was only instituted on the night before the Crucifixion, and as the apostles were apparently not competent to celebrate it until the day of Pentecost, we should not expect to find in the gospel histories any fuller reference than that which actually exists.

II. In the Acts of the Apostles the occasions are not many on which we might expect some mention of the Sacrament. The book is much more occupied with public discourses in the temple and in the synagogues, than with the internal worship of the Church. But it should be noted that when the worship of the Church comes to be mentioned, as at Troas, the Breaking of the Bread is referred to as a practice well understood and needing no explanation. It is assumed as the ordinary rule that on the first day of the week the disciples should come together to break bread.

III. The reticence of the Epistles is much more striking. It must be admitted that no theologian, or pastor, or director of souls in the present day could write at such length and on such subjects as are presented in the Epistles to the Romans and to the Ephesians, and in other Pauline Epistles, without making frequent reference to the central act of Christian worship. In St Peter's Epistles also, there are several passages in which a modern writer would almost certainly have made some allusion to the Sacrament. We can only say that the Holy Eucharist had not at that time become a subject of controversy, nor had men's minds been mystified by vain attempts to define the mode of God's operation. The faith on the subject was very simple and very clear, and stood in no particular need of apostolic exposition. The general practice was regular and consistent, and called for no special apostolic admonition. The idea of participating in a sacrifice by eating it was familiar enough. Christians did not doubt that the death of Christ was a full, perfect, and sufficient sacrifice, oblation and satisfaction for the sins of the whole world, and from well recognized analogies it followed that they should eat of the sacrifice in order to claim their part in these benefits. When a lamb or other clean beast had been sacrificed the worshippers could partake of the flesh. In regard to Christ's sacrifice He had given them the way to do the like, when He had consecrated the unbloody elements and said, This is My Body, This is My Blood. This appeared to be very clear and simple, and it was accepted without cavil by every Christian. Christ was present in the elements in the mode that made them his flesh to eat and his blood to drink, in a sense at least sufficient to constitute the feeding on the sacrifice. The idea of so defining his Presence as to make the Sacrament an object of worship, had not yet arisen. There was no controversy, and no need of explanation. Hence we can understand the very slight reference to the subject in letters which were not written as formal treatises on theology, but as counsels in current difficulties.

But simple as was the primitive view of the Holy Eucharist, it included the two great and essential ideas. If the recognized way to participate in a sacrifice and to claim its virtue for one's self was to eat of the victim, then the receiving of the Sacrament was to the worshipper the pleading before the throne of God of the merits of the great atonement on Calvary. And as the act of participation was not a mere ritual sign, but an actual eating and drinking, the truth was at once expressed that the faithful therein were feeding upon Christ for the strengthening and refreshing of their souls. Christ was to these primitive Christians the sacrificial Lamb of God that beareth and taketh away the sins of the world. He was also to them the Bread of Life, the Living Bread. "The Bread of God is that which cometh down from heaven and giveth Life unto the world."

Concerning the Holy Eucharist in these two aspects there is no dispute amongst us. As often as we receive it, we know that we are making before God the continual remembrance of the sacrifice of the death of Christ, and are claiming to participate in the benefits which flow therefrom. As often as we receive it, we know that our souls are being strengthened and refreshed by the body and blood of Christ, as our bodies are strengthened and refreshed by bread and wine; we eat the bread of God, we drink of the living fountain that springeth up unto life eternal.

Controversy about the Eucharist belongs altogether to a later period than that which we are now studying, and is almost entirely connected with the question, how is the sacrament to be treated when we are not receiving it? For the action of the devout communicant in receiving the sacrament is precisely the same whether he believe in an actual or a virtual presence. Reception means for him the feeding of his soul and participation in the merits of Christ's sacrifice, whether he hold any doctrine of transubstantiation or consubstantiation, or whether he rest upon the word and ordinance of Christ without staying to define the mode in which the divine promise is fulfilled. Hooker puts this very clearly when he writes:

"'This is my Body' and 'This is my Blood' being words of promise, since we all agree that by the sacrament Christ doth really and truly in us perform his promise, why do we vainly trouble ourselves with so fierce contentions, whether by consubstantiation or else by transubstantiation the sacrament itself be first possessed with Christ or no? a thing which no way can either further or hinder us howsoever it stand, because our participation in Christ in this sacrament dependeth on the co-operation of his omnipotent power which maketh it his body and blood to us, whether with change or without alteration of the element such as they imagine, we need not greatly to care or inquire.

The flood-gates of strife and contention were opened, when the Sacrament was put to another use, concerning which there was no word of Christ to afford guidance. For Christ gave no indication that it should be used in any other way than for reception. Where the Sacrament is reserved as an object of devotion in church, serious questions have to be faced. The modern Roman Church distinguishes three degrees [1] of worship: with which of these is the Blessed Sacrament to be approached? Or is the Eastern Church right in according only reverence and honour [2] to the elements, disallowing any worship of the sacramental presence, except in the celebration itself? Novel applications of the Sacra-

---

[1] (1) δουλεία; (2) ὑπερδουλεία; (3) λατρεία. A Roman Catholic handbook explains that (1) *dulia* is to be offered to the saints; (2) *hyperdulia*, to the Blessed Virgin; and (3) *latreia*, to God only.

[2] Τιμητικῇ προσκύνησις, but not λατρεία.

ment have prompted the desire for excessive definition, and that desire has resulted in dissension and division in the Church.

In apostolic days a purer air was breathed. The holiest rite of our religion had not yet become the battle-ground of contending parties. On the contrary it was the pledge and token of Unity. All observed it in the terms of our Lord's institution. He had established its sacrificial character when he said, *Do this*. It was, therefore, the rite in which the Church, for all and every one of her children, presented and pleaded before God the great atonement: the rite in which each faithful worshipper craved and claimed for himself participation in the efficacy of the sacrifice of the Cross. But He had also said: *Take, eat; Drink ye all; This is my body; This is my blood*. It was the taking into their own fallen but redeemed humanity something of Christ. It was for their souls an eating and a drinking, as essential to their spiritual life as food and drink to the bodily life. Christ had said it. None doubted. None disputed. All received it. Without controversy great is the mystery of Godliness—even Christ Himself.

HYMN OF APPROACH TO THE ALTAR.

Sinner, sin and shame confessing,
  Humble, contrite, penitent;
Toward the seat of mercy pressing:
  On the Saviour's love intent;
  Plead the one availing plea—
  Plead the death of Christ for thee.

Weak disciple, not relying
  On thyself—a broken reed—
But on God alone supplying
  Grace sufficient for thy need;
  Take the soul-sustaining food,
  Jesus' Body, Jesus' Blood.

Faithful Christian, making mention
  Of the ransom paid for thee,
Wondrous cost of man's redemption,
  Jesus' death upon the tree;
  Till He come, fulfil his word,
  Show the death of Christ the Lord.

Body one, by mystic union
  Of each member with the Head,
Share we all the sweet communion,
  All partaking of one Bread;
  Crowd the banquet as of old,
  Token of the faith we hold.

The Breaking of Bread at Troas.

Kneel we low in contemplation
  Of the wonders of the cross,
Jesus held in estimation,
  All beside accounted loss;
  Pledge we all our hearts to Christ—
  Celebrate the Eucharist.

Jesus, hail! we bow before Thee,
  In Thy holy Sacrament;
We approach Thee, we adore Thee,
  Knees low bending, hearts intent:
  Thee we worship, and in Thee
  God the Eternal Trinity.   Amen.

V.

THE EUCHARIST IN THE FIRST CENTURY.

"We have an altar, whereof they have no right to eat which serve the tabernacle."—*Hebrews*, xiii. 10.

WITHOUT entering into a discussion of the authorship of this epistle, we may note that it was certainly written by a Jew to Jews. The writer and those whom he addressed had, of course, been converted to Christ, but the questions treated of in the epistle are not those at issue between Christ and the world, but those between Christianity and Judaism. For aught of reference in the epistle, the heathen world might have been non-existent. The writer assumes that those who receive his letter are familiar with the Old Testament Scriptures, and with every detail of the Jewish ritual. The Jewish temple was still standing and the Mosaic sacrifices were still being offered. If the Hebrews were in danger of being carried about with divers and strange doctrines, these were not the speculations of gnostic or heathen philosophy, but rather pedantic applications of the law of Moses—minute rules about clean and unclean meats—such as the writer sweeps aside with the assertion: "It is a good thing that the heart be established with grace, not with meats which have not profited them that have been occupied therein." The writer desires to call back the attention of the Hebrew Christians from the Jewish sacrifices, which were so soon to cease, to the one great sacrifice of which they were but types, namely, that which was offered upon the altar of the Cross of Calvary. To this sacrifice he asserts that the obsolete ceremonies of the tabernacle afford no access. "We have an altar, whereof they have no right to eat which serve the tabernacle."

In the Jewish ritual there were different ways in which the worshipper was commanded to claim his part in the efficacious virtue of a sacrifice. Sometimes he was to express his identity with the victim by laying his hand upon its head. On other occasions, a much more significant form was used: the worshipper was actually to eat of the flesh of the victim, whilst another part was offered and burned upon the altar of

God. This is of extreme interest to us, for it shows us how significant our Lord's words about the eating of his flesh must have seemed to the disciples, when once they had come to regard his death upon the Cross as the sacrifice, oblation, and satisfaction for the sins of the whole world. To eat the flesh of the sacrifice was equivalent to participation in the virtue and merits of the sacrifice.

This accepted principle is assumed in the passage before us. "We have an altar, whereof they have no right to eat which serve the tabernacle."

When he says, "We have an altar," I do not see any reference to the material structure on which we are accustomed to consecrate the Blessed Sacrament. The words, "we have an altar," are equivalent, by a common use of language to the words "we have a sacrifice," and the reference is undoubtedly to the oblation of Christ upon the cross as a sacrifice for the sins of the world. "We have an altar" is the proper and appropriate text, not so much for Maundy Thursday as for Good Friday.

But I think that the words which follow have an undoubted reference to the Blessed Sacrament. For I do not see how the writer could have spoken of the right to "eat" of the altar unless Christians as well as Jews were accustomed, by eating, to participate in the sacrifice. Given, that the altar refers not to the Holy Table, but to the cross and to the atonement wrought thereon, he could not speak of our eating of that sacrifice unless a sacrament of eating had been instituted as the mode by which we were to claim our part in the great sacrifice once made.

We considered on two former Sunday mornings the Breaking of the Bread at Jerusalem immediately after the day of Pentecost, and the Breaking of the Bread at Troas some twenty-five years later. I have now, in fact, called your attention incidentally to all the passages in the New Testament in which direct reference is made to that highest act of Christian worship, the showing of the Lord's death till he come.

But the references to Christian worship in early times are not restricted to the canonical scriptures. If we wish to trace the development of our service from the beginning, we must study the accounts given by successive Christian writers, and we must note also the references which even profane historians incidentally make to the practices of the Christians.

But the materials for such study are very meagre until we reach a later century. The secular writers of the day knew nothing whatever of the interior practices of the Church; and when we refer to such Christian writings outside the New Testament, as have been thought to belong to the first century, our search for a word or expression which may throw light on the mode of Christian worship, is disappointing in the extreme.

Turn, for example, to the epistle of Barnabas. Though we cannot accept it as a genuine epistle of the companion of St Paul, many critics attribute it to the first century. At the latest it belongs to the first half of the second century. Its main object is to show how the Jewish sacrifices have been fulfilled in Christ, and the Jewish worship superseded by that of the Gospel. The writer interprets minute details of the old law as prefiguring Christian rites. Yet he says practically nothing about the rites of Christian worship thus prefigured. In one place he speaks of the duty of coming more holily and nearer "to his altar." In another place he indicates the observance of the Lord's day, saying, "We observe the eighth day with gladness in which Jesus rose from the dead." But his silence as to the central act of Christian worship is as marked as that which we noted in all but one of the canonical epistles. It is, perhaps, due to excessive caution lest any account of the Christian mysteries might fall into pagan hands.

Equally disappointing is the search when we turn to other writers of the century to look for details of Christian worship.

The Epistle of Clement to the Corinthians was probably written in the year 95, still within the lifetime of St John. This document does not contain any account of the celebration of the Eucharist, but the writer strongly insists that men are to make their offerings and service to God at the appointed times, and he says God has ordained both where and by what persons the services are to be performed; and in this connection he insists strongly on the prerogative of the clergy, after the analogy of those of the Jewish worship; for, he adds, "the chief priest has his proper services, and to the priests their proper place is assigned; and to the Levites appertain their proper ministries;

the layman is confined to what is appointed for laymen. Let each one of you make his Eucharist to God in his own station with a good conscience, with reverent demeanour, not transgressing the appointed rule of his service." And in the next chapter of his epistle he continues: "Christ was from God, and the apostles from Christ ... and the apostles appointed the first fruits of their conversions to be bishops and deacons."

I have ventured to interpret the Greek word εὐχαριστείτω as meaning "let him take his part in the service of the Eucharist." Some would simply render it "let him give thanks"; but it is plain from the context that the reference is to the public worship of the Church, and to a service ordered with strict regularity and with regard to spiritual office. Such a reference can only be to the Breaking of the Bread.[1] It is

---

[1] Bishop Lightfoot says: "The allusion here is plainly to the public services of the Church, where order had been violated. Thus *Eucharistia* will refer chiefly, though not solely, to the principal act of Christian thanksgiving, the celebration of the Lord's Supper, which at a later date was almost exclusively termed *Eucharistia*. The usage of Clement is probably midway between that of St Paul, where no such appropriation of the term appears, and that of the Ignatian Epistles and of Justin, where it is specially so applied.

certainly remarkable that no clearer allusion to sacramental worship can be found in an epistle twice as long as the Epistle to the Hebrews, in which references to our approach to God in the appointed mode and in the right spirit are by no means wanting.

The only extant document attributed to the first century which contains any account of the celebration of the Eucharist is the short treatise known as the Διδαχή or *Teaching of the Twelve Apostles.* Even if we allow the later date to which Dr Biggs assigns the composition, there is every indication that the account of Christian worship imbedded in it belongs to the earliest age. But such trustworthy scholars as Bishop Lightfoot and Dr Taylor have no hesitation in assigning the whole composition to the first century. If they are right, it was written in the lifetime of St John, and no earlier account of Christian worship is extant outside the canon of the New Testament. Before I read the passage to you, I would point out that though it is sometimes difficult to decide whether the Greek word εὐχαριστία refers to the Sacrament, or to an ordinary act of thanksgiving apart from the Sacrament, there is no such difficulty here. For the injunction that the unbaptized may not partake, clearly indicates that what is being discussed is not a thanksgiving over ordinary food, but is the very Sacramental Eucharist itself.

The passage is as follows:

And as touching the feast of Thanksgiving, thus give ye thanks:

First, concerning the cup, We thank thee, O our Father, for the holy vine of thy child David, which thou hast made known to us by thy child Jesus. Thine be the glory for ever. And concerning the broken bread, We thank thee, O our Father, for the life and knowledge which thou hast made known to us by thy child Jesus. Thine be the glory for ever. As this broken bread was once scattered in grains upon the mountains, and being gathered together became one; so let thy church be gathered together from the ends of the earth unto thy kingdom. For thine is the glory and the power through Jesus Christ for ever.

And let none eat or drink of your feast of Thanksgiving, but such as have been baptized in the name of the Lord; for concerning this the Lord hath said, *Give not that which is holy to the dogs.*

And after being filled, thus give ye thanks:

We thank thee, holy Father, for thy holy name which thou hast made to dwell in our hearts, and for the knowledge and faith and immortality which thou hast made known to us by thy child Jesus. Thine be the glory for ever. Thou, O almighty Sovereign, didst create all things for thy name's sake, and gavest men food and drink to enjoy, that they might give thanks unto thee; but to us thou didst graciously give spiritual food and drink and life eternal, through thy child. Before all things we give thanks to thee for that thou art mighty. Thine is the glory for ever. Remember, O Lord, thy church to deliver her from all evil and to perfect her in thy love; and gather her together from the four winds, her that is sanctified unto thy kingdom which thou didst prepare for her. For thine is the power and the glory for ever. Let grace come, and this world pass away. Hosanna to the God of David. If any is holy let him come; if any is not, let him repent. Maranatha. Amen.

But suffer ye the prophets to give thanks as pleaseth them.[1]

In these directions for the celebration of the Holy Eucharist in the first century, you will observe that nothing is said about the consecration of the elements. I think that this is to be accounted for as an instance of the reluctance which the early Church felt to commit her most sacred formulæ to writing. We find exactly the same thing two hundred years later, when St Cyril, in explaining the service to those who had just been admitted to communion, dwells at

---

[1] Taylor's translation. I should have ventured to use the term *Eucharist*, in place of *Feast of Thanksgiving*.

length on what precedes and follows, but passes over the Consecration itself with the words: "Then, after the spiritual sacrifice is perfected." This reluctance to divulge matters pertaining to the faith was very real, and must always be taken into account in interpreting the records of the early Church.

You will observe also, that although the dominant note is Thanksgiving, yet the celebration is made an occasion of Intercession: "Remember, O Lord, thy Church, to deliver her and to perfect her." You will note also that the sacramental feeding of the soul is carefully emphasized: "Thou gavest men food and drink to enjoy, but to us thou didst graciously give spiritual food and drink through Thy Child." At the same time there is not the slightest hint of any adoration towards the consecrated elements. In fact, the first trace of such adoration does not occur till a much later age.

It does not appear that at the period under our consideration, the Eucharistic prayers had taken any prescribed form. The form given in the passage that I have read to you, appears to be little more than an example of such a thanksgiving as might fitly be offered, and in the concluding words the right is reserved to the

The Eucharist in the First Century. 89

prophets, if any be present, of offering an extempore thanksgiving to any extent they choose: the prophets being those who were still exercising some of the extraordinary gifts of Pentecost.

It is rather remarkable that while the presence of a prophet is provided for, apparently as something exceptional, nothing is said about the necessity of there being a priest to consecrate the sacrament. But if anyone imagines that at this time this function could be discharged by laymen, I would remind him of the passage already referred to, in which Clement insists on the prerogative of the clergy in the public services of the Church.

I will not weary you with any longer quotation. In the passages which we have cited, we have contemporary evidence as to the main characteristics of the Divine Service towards the close of the first century. Though there was probably not yet a written and authorized liturgy, the Eucharistic prayers were already of a very definite character, and they were offered with much decency and order, the several ranks of the ministry having their proper functions clearly defined. The typical character of the outward and visible sign was duly recognized; the thanksgiving over the wine was for "the Holy Vine of David," and that over the bread was for "the life and knowledge" suggested by our Lord's title as the Bread of Life. God's goodness in creation was acknowledged in the simplest and most natural terms, but the gift to the faithful was described as "spiritual food and drink, and life eternal." A prayer for the extension and unity of the church preceded communion, and this great intercession was renewed at the close of the service.

Substantially the celebration in the first century was identical with the celebration to-day. But the more we study these ancient records the deeper becomes the impression that a great change of proportion has taken place. More prominence is now given to the fact that our souls are strengthened and refreshed by the body and blood of Christ as our bodies are by bread and wine, and less prominence in proportion is given to the fact that in receiving the Sacrament we are claiming our part in the sacrifice of the Cross. The idea that we participate in the efficacy of a sacrifice by eating the flesh of the victim, was a familiar commonplace to

The Eucharist in the First Century. 91

the early Christians: it is much less familiar to us. To our minds the act of eating and drinking suggests sustenance and refreshment much more naturally than it suggests participation in the sacrifice. Indeed the latter idea has become so far obscured that many people think that they can, in some sacramental sense, plead the sacrifice, though they do not receive the Sacrament. Perhaps the change of proportion is best illustrated by considering the different thoughts which a Christian of the first century and a Christian of the nineteenth century would attach to such phrases as "the altar whereof we eat," or "our being partakers of the altar." The early Christian would at once have thought of the altar of the Cross: partaking of the altar would have meant to him participation in the Sacrifice of Calvary; whereas the modern worshipper is more ready to apply the phrase to the material altar, almost as if the sacrifice were complete within the four walls of the Church. In mediæval and modern times language has been used which seems to imply that the worshipper need look no further than the earthly sanctuary: or if he is to look beyond it his gaze is to be carried upward, that he may join in worship with angels and archangels, and with all the company of

Heaven. But to the primitive Christian there was another background to the sanctuary, even Calvary itself with the great tragedy enacted thereupon. Christ is present in the Church to feed our souls, but the sacrifice of which we eat is not wrought within these walls, but, once for all, on the green hill far away where the immaculate Lamb was slain.

I am not alleging any change of doctrine, but I do allege a change in the proportions in which the different aspects of the truth are brought into prominence. And if anyone doubts this change he is confronted by the manifest change of practice, contrasting the regular communions of the first century with the irregular and occasional communions of the present day. If communion be thought of mainly as spiritual food for our souls, it may be open to argument how often, considering the smallness of our spiritual capacity, we ought to receive these gifts: but if communion be thought of as the appointed means of participation in that one Sacrifice, by which alone we can acceptably approach the throne of God, then we can understand the mind of the primitive Christian, who would not think of keeping the Lord's Day without the reception of the Sacrament.

My brethren, these historical investigations will be of spiritual service to us all if they lead us to be more intelligent communicants, our faith and our devotion being guided, not by the catch-words of party, which are so lightly acquired, but by the reverent contemplation of our Lord's intention, and by the careful study of the place which the Blessed Sacrament occupied in the worship of the faithful, from the time when the apostles themselves were living to direct the Church.

The honest study of the subject must have one immediate result—to make you utterly dissatisfied with a life which does not unceasingly claim participation in the great oblation of the Cross; it must lead you to regular and habitual Communion, and therein to a fuller appreciation of that great action of atonement in which the Lamb of God hath borne the burden of the sins of the world.

VI.

THE EUCHARIST IN THE SECOND CENTURY.

"Lo, I am with you alway, even unto the end of the world."—*St Matthew*, xxviii. 20.

MY mind is fixed upon a day in the history of the Church, when the promise of the text must have come home to men's hearts with peculiar power. I am not thinking of the day of the Ascension, though the great joy of that day must have been compounded of the strong faith in the abiding presence of the Master. My thoughts range onward to another day when, but for this promise, the minds of the faithful must have been fraught with dismay. I am thinking of the death-day of the last of the apostles, when St John, the beloved disciple, passed to his rest.

The other apostles had long before proved faithful unto death. But the faithful in the Church were watching every day for the return

The Eucharist in the Second Century. 95

of Christ, and were fondly trusting to the inference which they drew from a literal interpretation of the Lord's words concerning St John: "If I will that he tarry till I come, what is that to thee?" They hoped that until the return of Christ to gather in his own, they should enjoy always the presence and the counsel of one, at least, of the favoured band, who had known Him, face to face, in the days of his ministry; who had heard his gracious words, and could tell of the irresistible sweetness of his presence; who, moreover, had seen Him after his resurrection, and had received the instruction of the great forty days in the things concerning his kingdom; who had been witnesses of his final withdrawal into the heavens, and had experienced the power of the rushing, mighty wind of Pentecost and the tongues of fire.

And now the last of them was gone and Jesus had not come: and the outlook must have been dark indeed, if they had not had the promise, "Lo, I am with you alway, even unto the end of the world." But herein they found assurance. The apostolic commission was not to die out with the apostles—for though all flesh is as grass, and the glory of man as the flower of grass, yet the word of the Lord endureth for ever. "Lo, I am with you alway, even unto the end of the world."

The passing away of the apostles must have had a great effect upon the Church. Hitherto, they had looked up to chief pastors whose commission had been anterior to the Church. For the future, the Church herself must beget her rulers, and this fact alone emphasized the conception of the Church as a living body in union with Christ. Never before had so great significance attached to the promise—never before had it been so strongly recognized as, in fact, essential to the very being of the Church: "Lo, I am with you alway, even unto the end of the world."

The death of St John was thus an epoch in the history of the Church. It synchronized very closely with the end of the first century, so that we may think of the second century as inaugurating new conditions in the Church's life.

In the present course of sermons we are concentrating our attention on historical evidence as to the public services of the Church, and we do not proceed far in the second century before we come to some very striking allusions to our subject in a profane author.

In the year 112 Trajan was emperor of Rome and Pliny was governor of the Roman province of Bithynia. Pliny found his province overrun by Christians to such an extent that the temples of the national religion were almost deserted. Being determined to remedy this state of things, he began by calling upon all suspected persons to offer incense to the national gods and to the image of Cæsar. When they refused and avowed themselves Christians he ordered some to be put to death: others, who had the rights of Roman citizens, he proposed to send to the capital. But the accounts which he heard of the Christians from some apostates, and from two deaconesses whom he put to torture, caused him some misgiving, and he wrote to the emperor for instructions. He reports to the emperor that those whom he has examined have given the following account of Christianity:

"They affirmed that the whole sum of their fault or error was this: that they were in the habit of meeting on a fixed day before dawn, and of reciting alternately a hymn to Christ as to a God, and of binding themselves by an oath or sacrament, not to some wickedness, but that they would abstain from theft, and robbery, and adultery, and would not break their word, nor withhold a deposit when reclaimed. After this (they said) it was their custom to separate, and to come together later for a common meal, which, however, was quite harmless. And from this meal they had desisted after my edict, in which, in accordance with your command, I had forbidden club-meetings."

There is no doubt that the "stated day" mentioned in this very interesting account was Sunday. But as there was at that time no general cessation of business on Sunday, the only possible time for the worship of the Church must have been early in the morning before work began, or in the evening when work was done. In the first century we found that they came together in the evening to break bread. Now in the second century it appears that they meet twice in the day. In the early morning they recite a hymn to Christ as a God, and they take a pledge against all wickedness. Some have thought that this statement about the oath was founded on some report of the baptismal vows, and that the Eucharist was still celebrated at the evening meeting. But we can hardly think that these Christians would have given up the Eucharist in consequence of Pliny's edict

The Eucharist in the Second Century.

against club-meetings (*hetærias*, ἑταιρείας). We must rather conclude that the oath or pledge, for which Pliny uses the word *sacramentum*, was none other than that obligation to holiness which was sealed and renewed in every Communion: that the early morning meeting, at which they recited the hymn to Christ, was, in fact, the celebration of the Eucharist, and that the evening meeting was for the common meal which they properly gave up when Pliny issued his edict against social clubs.

In view of the change of hour for the Holy Eucharist, some writers have assumed very strangely that the evening hour gradually became later and later (just as the meeting at Troas was prolonged when St Paul continued his sermon to midnight), until the time of assembly passed from the late evening to the early morning. But it is obvious that this hypothesis would account for a change from Sunday night to *Monday* morning: but what actually occurred was a change from Sunday night to *Sunday* morning, and this must have been deliberately made. Up to this point the Agapé and the Eucharist were held almost as one feast; the Eucharist was apparently an episode in the

Agapé. But now, perhaps in consequence of such irregularities as St Paul had to denounce at Corinth, the Eucharist is celebrated in the early morning, and the love-feast, if it is held at all, is in the evening.

Bishop Lightfoot has established beyond gainsaying the authenticity of the letters written by St Ignatius about the year 110, on his way from Antioch to Rome to suffer martyrdom. He had been sentenced to be thrown to the wild beasts. The letters are addressed to different Churches, and in six out of the seven, in view of some tendency to independence and secession, the writer passionately insists on the authority of the bishop. If the Christian community be divided, those who remain with the bishop are to be deemed the true Church. Do nothing (he says) without the bishop. Apart from the bishop it is not lawful either to baptize or to celebrate the Agapé. From his citing Baptism and the Agapé as the two principal ministrations of the Church, we conclude that Ignatius regarded the Agapé as including the Eucharist. If in Bithynia the Agapé was first separated from the Eucharist and then abandoned altogether, it would seem that elsewhere the Agapé first included the

Eucharist and then became entirely merged in it. Ignatius goes on to caution the Church at Smyrna against those who taught that our Lord's human body was only flesh in appearance and not in reality, and in argument with them he uses language which almost implies a material presence in the Eucharist. These heretics, he says, "abstain from the Eucharist and from the public prayers, because they confess not that the Eucharist is the flesh of our Saviour Jesus Christ, which flesh suffered for our sins, and which the Father of his goodness raised from the dead." At a later point we shall have to consider the sense in which even stronger language than this was used.

I will now turn to the testimony of a Christian writer about the middle of the century. It was probably in the year 148 that Justin Martyr addressed to the Emperor his apology for Christianity. He shows that the faith and worship of Christians are reasonable, and tend to good order: and are in no way opposed to the cause of civil government. As Justin is writing to a heathen emperor, he naturally will not reveal the more sacred mysteries of Christianity, but he speaks very plainly of the religious practice of his time. He thus defines the general character of Christian worship.

We worship the creator of the universe, whom we assert to have no need of sacrifices of blood, and libations, and incense, but whom we praise to the best of our power with the reasonable service of prayer and thanksgiving, in all our oblations, having been instructed that the only service that is worthy of Him is not to consume by fire what He has given us for our sustenance, but to apply it to our own benefit and to those who are in need . . . . offering Him solemnities and hymns . . . . and putting up prayers that we may have a resurrection to incorruptibility through our faith in Him.

Further on, Justin describes how new members are initiated into the Christian Church:

They are taught to pray and beg God with fasting to grant them forgiveness of their former sins: and we pray and fast with them. Then we bring them where there is water, and after the same manner of regeneration as we also were regenerated ourselves they are regenerated. . . .

After thus washing him who has professed and given his assent, we bring him to those who are called brethren, where they are assembled together, to offer prayers in common. . . . We salute one another with a kiss when we have concluded the prayers; then is brought to the president of the brethren bread and a cup of water and mixed wine, which he receives, and offers up praise and glory. . . . When he has concluded the prayers and thanksgiving all the people express their assent by saying "Amen;" and when the president has celebrated, and all the people have assented, they whom we call deacons give to each of those who are present a portion of the Eucharistic bread and wine and water, and carry them to those who are absent. And this food is called by us the Eucharist, of which no one is allowed to partake but he who believes the truth of our doctrines, and has been washed in the laver for the forgiveness of sins and for regeneration, and who so lives as Christ has directed. For we do not receive them as ordinary food or ordinary drink. But as by the Word of God Jesus Christ our Saviour was made flesh, and had both flesh and blood for our salvation, so also the food which was blessed by the prayer of the word which proceeded from him, and from which our flesh and blood are nourished by assimilation, is the flesh and blood of that Jesus which was made flesh. For the apostles in their memoirs, which are called gospels, have thus delivered to us what was enjoined on them, that Jesus took bread and gave thanks and said, "Do this in remembrance of me: this is my body," and that after the same manner He took the cup and gave thanks and said, "This is my blood." . . . And over all things of which we partake we bless the Creator of all things through his Son Jesus Christ and through the Holy Spirit. And on the day called Sunday all who live in cities or in the country gather together in one place, and the records of the apostles or the writings of the prophets are read as long as time permits. Then the reader concludes, and the president verbally instructs and exhorts us to the imitation of these good things. Then we all rise together and offer prayers. And as we have before said, when we have finished the prayer, bread and wine and water are brought, and the president in like manner offers prayers and thanksgiving with all his might, and the people assent, saying "Amen," and there is a distribution to each, and a participation in the Eucharistic elements, and portions are sent to those who are not present by the deacons. And those who have means and are willing give as each thinks fit, and the collection is placed in the hands of the president, who assists the orphans and widows and those who are in want through sickness or any other cause, and those who are in prison, and the strangers sojourning among us, and, in a word, he takes care of all who are in any need.

These passages set before us with considerable detail the central act of Christian worship a little more than one hundred years after the Crucifixion.

I. First, we note that a celebration of Holy Communion followed an adult baptism, so that the sacred food might be the first to pass the lips of the newly illuminated. The fast before baptism is much more ancient and of much greater authority than the fast before Communion, and the latter seems to have originated in the former. Justin tells us that not only the candidate for baptism fasted, but the whole Church fasted with him, making the latter dependent on the former. And the earliest canon which enjoins a fast before Communion enjoins it particularly on the newly baptized and with less emphasis on others. But this custom belongs to a later century, and must not detain us now.

II. We observe that in the second century, as in the first, Holy Communion was celebrated every Sunday. It was the Lord's service on the Lord's day.

III. In the first passage quoted from Justin he says that we are to offer God πόμπας καὶ ὕμνους, which we have rendered "solemnities and hymns." But there is much doubt about the meaning of the first word, πόμπας, "pomps." It was used by the Greeks and Romans to denote solemn processions, but it is extremely unlikely that Justin uses it in this sense. Some think that it denotes the rites and ritual that accompany a sacrament, but at the very least the expression implies that services were rendered with dignity and decency and order, according to some stated ritual.

IV. Incense was not used. Justin classes it with the sacrifices of blood and the libations which God does not require : and half a century later, Tertullian speaks of it in even stronger terms of disparagement. But the kiss of peace was one of the ceremonies of the celebration.

V. You will observe that the weekly offertory accompanies the celebration. This was first ordained by St Paul in his Epistle to the Corinthians: "On the first day of the week let every one of you lay by him in store as God hath prospered him." Reference to the practice as forming part of the Communion Service is very rare, and we read with the greater interest Justin's clear and distinct mention of it. And in this connection we may note Justin's enlightened words on the consecration of objects to the service of God. I sometimes meet with those who think that when a carpet or a hanging or some other object has served its purpose in church and is no longer required for sacred use it is better to burn it—or to put it by and consecrate it to uselessness—rather than apply it to any common or secular use. Justin takes a higher view when he says that "the only service worthy of God is not to consume by fire what is given to us for our sustenance, but to apply it to our own benefit or to that of those who are in need."

VI. There was no such practice as what is now called non-communicating attendance. All present received the Sacrament, and it was taken by the deacons to those who were absent. Every Christian as a matter of course communicated every Sunday, even if he could not be present at the celebration.

VII. The Sacrament was reserved for the immediate communion of the sick or of others who were unavoidably absent. In process of time this led to certain abuses. Sometimes, instead of reverently receiving the Sacrament when the deacon brought it, a person would put it by in an ark or casket to be subsequently received, or, as was sometimes the case, to be treated superstitiously as a charm. But this was not the intention of the Church. The intention seems to have been precisely that which was revived in our own Prayer Book in 1549 and is probably lawful still. That book provided that if the celebrating priest had notice of a sick person who desired to receive the Sacrament, he might set aside sufficient of the consecrated elements for the purpose, and as soon as he conveniently could, after the conclusion of the service, he was to go and administer the same to the sick person.[1] I suppose that no one in our own branch of the Church would ever have objected to such a practice, if the Sacrament reserved for the sick had not been made the means of reviving a mediæval superstition.

VIII. Note again, that there was a sermon or exhortation at the celebration of the Eucharist, and that whatever form of consecration was used the president was accustomed to enlarge upon it in his own words, *i.e.*, in extempore prayer.

IX. Note also the allusion to the natural effect of bread and wine in nourishing our body as

---

[1] The rubric at the end of the Communion Service which treats of the Bread and Wine that remains unconsecrated, and any that may remain of that which was consecrated, assigning the former to the curate's own use, but requiring the latter to be reverently eaten and drunk in the Church, is plainly directed, not against superstition, but against irreverence. The rubric is concerned with that which remains over when all legitimate purposes are fulfilled. The priest first communicates those who are present: then, if need be, he sets aside a sufficiency for the sick person who is awaiting communion at home; and then, if any remain, it must be dealt with as the rubric directs.

affording some analogy to the effect of Communion upon our souls. References to this analogy are very rare in early writings, though the thought is familiar enough to ourselves from the prominence given to it in the Church Catechism, where we are taught that our souls are strengthened and refreshed by the body and blood of Christ, as our bodies are (naturally) by bread and wine.

Surely such a study as we are now engaged in tends to illuminate for us the promise of the text. For it leads us to realize the substantial identity of our own worship in the Church of England to-day with that which was offered in the Early Church in the earliest centuries of the Christian era. Such a continuity of worship bears witness to Jesus Christ—the same yesterday, to-day, and for ever—and to his gracious promise, " Lo, I am with you alway, even unto the end of the world."

He is with his Church to-day as surely as in the days of the Apostles—to guide her unto all truth. Yet his presence with the Church—like his presence with the individual—is effective only in proportion to the disposition to receive Him and to hear his voice. If the Church or any branch of the Church ceases to ask, "What hath God spoken?" there will be little experience of his presence. But when the Church turns to the divine testimony, to the word of God, and desires the guiding light of the Spirit thereupon, she shall not be disappointed, she shall find the truth of the promise of her Lord, "Lo! I am with you alway, even unto the end of the world."

And to each separate soul the promise is made good in the hour of devout Communion. The Sacrament is the Sacrament of his presence. As the beloved St John lay on his breast at supper, so the devout communicant is resting on an ever present Saviour, and hears his word of assurance whispered in the depth of the heart,
 Lo, I am with you alway, even unto the end of the world."

VII.

THE EUCHARIST IN THE THIRD CENTURY.

"Ye cannot be partakers of the Lord's table and of the table of devils."—1 *Cor.* x. 21.

ST PAUL appeals to the Jewish law, that those who ate of the sacrifices became thereby participators in the action wrought upon the altar. "Behold Israel after the flesh," he says, "Are not they which eat of the sacrifices partakers of the altar?"

So he regards Holy Communion as a pledge of allegiance to Christ, an allegiance which must be whole and undivided, for the Lord our God is a jealous God, and brooks no rival on his Throne within us. We are to serve Him with all our heart, and mind, and soul, and strength. Therefore saith St James, "The friendship of the world is enmity with God, for the spirit which He hath given us jealously desireth us." It is the reiteration of our Lord's own words, "Ye cannot serve God and Mammon."

This aspect of Holy Communion was very prominent in the early centuries, when Christians were set in the midst of heathen, and were called upon sometimes in the ordinary courtesies of social life, and sometimes as a specific test of their loyalty to the national gods, to eat of the things which had been offered to idols. In the chapter before us St Paul deals with questions of conscience thus arising, and he settles such questions with what we should call much liberal common sense. He reminds Christians that an idol is nothing in the world, and that no essential character either of good or evil is attached to meat by the mere fact of its having been offered in the idol's temple. The Christian, therefore, need not be scrupulous when meat is set before him, to inquire whether it have been so offered or not. He need not ask any such question for conscience sake; for to his own conscience the meat is simply the gift of God for his sustenance, under the rule that the earth is the Lord's and the fulness thereof. But if he be told that it has been offered to an idol he must not eat it. For his eating it with that knowledge would inevitably be understood as an act of fellowship in the idolatrous worship, and the weak brother might be led by such an example to justify himself in a practical denial of Christ.

In our own times no such literal application of the text arises. Yet there are idolatries enough against which we must be on our guard in the world around us, and there are devilries enough to which we must give no countenance, no tacit connivance, if we would be true to our Lord and Master. "Ye cannot be partakers of the Lord's Table and of the table of devils"—is a warning full of significance for us and for all. It might well be written in letters of fire across the entrance to the sanctuary, as a flaming sword to guard the way to the tree of life. It suggests the proclamation in which in ancient liturgies the unworthy were bidden depart before the celebration of the holy mysteries : it suggests to us the warning in our own Communion Service, "If any of you be a blasphemer of God, an hinderer or slanderer of his Word, an adulterer, or be in malice, or envy, or in any other grievous crime, repent you of your sins, or else come not to that holy Table." "Ye cannot be partakers of the Lord's Table and of the table of devils."

In the Christian literature of the third century

we find many allusions to the Blessed Sacrament in the aspect in which St Paul presents it here.

St Cyprian, writing in the year 251, relates a number of portents which attended unworthy attempts to partake of the Lord's table. Apart from their direct application these legends are very interesting, as incidentally throwing much light upon the prevailing thought, and upon the practices of that time.

He first tells of an infant left by Christian parents with a heathen nurse. The babe was not able to eat meat, but they gave it some bread steeped in wine which had been used in the heathen sacrifice. Afterwards the mother brought the child to the celebration of the Eucharist, but it was convulsed with weeping, as not able now to endure the Christian sacrifice: and when the deacon brought the Sacrament for those who were present to receive, the infant compressed its lips; and when it was forced to receive there followed, says St Cyprian, a sobbing and a vomiting: the Eucharist was not able to remain in a body and mouth which had been polluted. Another of maturer years, who had saved her life by participating in a heathen sacrifice, came to the Eucharist, and the holy bread became to her, as it were, a sword. She was seized with an agony and phrenzy as if she had taken some deadly poison. Another woman attempting with desecrated hands to open the casket in which she kept the Sacrament, a fire immediately rose from the box, so that she dare not touch it. A man who had defiled himself, adventuring secretly to receive the Sacrament, was disabled from eating the Holy Thing, and on opening his hands discovered that he held a cinder.

The spiritual application of these stories is quite clear. St Cyprian himself draws the inference that "the Lord withdraws when He is denied," and that "what unfit persons receive cannot profit them unto salvation, since the saving grace turns into ashes when holiness departs." "Ye cannot be partakers of the Lord's Table and of the table of devils."

Incidentally the narrative shows that in the third century infants were communicated, though there is reason to believe that they only received the Sacrament once after their baptism, and not subsequently until they came to years of discretion. There is reference also to the casket or ark in which private persons kept the Holy Sacrament for reception at home. This custom seems to have been almost universal, and altogether uncondemned in the third century. It is repeatedly alluded to by Tertullian, who wrote about fifty years earlier. In one place Tertullian suggests that scrupulous people who will not communicate at the celebration on Good Friday because it would break their fast, should attend the service and take the Sacrament home with them, to receive it in the evening when the fast is over. This is the first trace in history of the corrupt practice which became so prevalent in a later age, of putting asunder the two things which Christ had joined together—the Eucharistic worship and the reception of the Sacrament. In another place Tertullian, enlarging on the inconvenience of a Christian woman marrying a heathen man, urges that the husband would want to know what it was that the wife partakes of *ante omnem cibum*, "before all food," or as Bishop Kingdon renders it, "before every meal." Whether it were taken only in the morning, or in connection with every meal, the reference is to the consecrated portion kept in the ark for what we may call domestic Communion.

We gather from the chapter before us that meats that had been offered to idols were sold in the market and used in social feasts. There is a certain beauty in the connection thus established between religion and common life: and we should be sorry if such a suggestive association were confined exclusively to idolatrous worship. But if we look beneath the surface of some of the customs and courtesies of life, we may find sacred memorials of our holy religion where they are, perhaps, little suspected.

Last Friday at evensong, we heard Boaz salute his work-people with the benediction: "The Lord be with you," and they responded: "The Lord bless thee." The forms with which we now commonly greet our friends have a less sacred sound, but the scholar is aware that they are abbreviations of ancient formularies, in which friend invoked upon friend the divine benediction. Our familiar good-day is but the corruption of the sacred salutation, God give you a good day. Thus, in the most familiar greetings, we are echoing the priestly benediction of the Church; not merely expressing our own good will towards our friend, but invoking upon him, in solemn prayer, the effectual blessing of God.

And in like manner our grace before meat is an echo of the Eucharist. He took bread and blessed and brake it, and gave it to them when

He instituted the Holy Sacrament: but again at Emmaus, He took bread and blessed it, and brake and gave to them when (as we must infer) He was *not* celebrating the Sacrament. But the two actions were closely associated. And so it would seem that the early Christians in saying grace were, at least, joining in spirit in the Blessed Sacrament; and it is quite possible that Bishop Kingdon's interpretation of Tertullian's words is correct, and that, in the third century, a devout woman, having the Sacrament reserved in her ark, would taste it before every meal in remembrance of Christ.

The association of the Eucharist with the domestic meal is further illustrated by another passage in St Cyprian. It occurs in a letter in which St Cyprian is insisting upon the use of the mixed chalice in settlement of what will probably appear to you a very curious question. The very fact that such a question could have arisen shows very clearly how far was the ritual of the Church from being rigidly defined even in the matter of the most Holy Sacrament.

You may have remarked in the careful reading of your Bible that the apostles, writing of the Blessed Sacrament, never mention what was in the cup. In fact, if it were not for our Lord's

The Eucharist in the Third Century. 119

declaration that He would drink no more of the fruit of the vine, we should be bound to admit that the Holy Scriptures nowhere indicate that wine was used in the Sacrament. St Paul speaks of the bread which we break, and of the cup which we bless. He does not mention the contents of the cup. So again he says, "let a man eat of that bread and drink of that cup." The Sacrament is described in the Acts of the Apostles as the Breaking of the Bread, but there is no corresponding reference to the wine: and St Paul's imagery of our being all partakers of the One Bread, is followed in the earliest Christian writings, but no similar teaching is drawn from the wine. It is, therefore, not a great surprise to find that in the early Christian centuries, while bread was universally allowed to be a necessary element in the Sacrament, there was considerable doubt about the necessity of wine. The bread must be broken and the cup must be blessed, whatever the cup might contain. There were many Christians who celebrated with water, remembering that as Christ had called Himself the Bread of Life, so He had described Himself as the giver of Living Water.

It fell to the lot of St Cyprian to settle these differences. He decided, chiefly on mystical grounds, that in consecrating the cup, water alone cannot be offered, neither wine alone. He insisted on the mixture, in which he thought the wine represented the blood of Christ, and the water the people: "so that when in the cup water is mingled with the wine, his people are united to Christ, and the multitude of believers are united and conjoined with Him in whom they believe." He probably was on safer ground when he argued elsewhere that the sacrifice must be offered as Christ Himself instituted and offered it.[1]

He goes on to answer the excuses which some had made for the use of water instead of wine. He asks: "Does anyone soothe himself with this consideration, that although in the morning water alone is seen to be offered, yet when we come to supper we offer the cup mixed?" This

---

[1] Those who have used what is called "non-intoxicating wine" or "the unfermented juice of the grape" in the celebration of the Sacrament may be judged guilty of great irregularity in disregarding the settled rule of the Church. But we shall hesitate to say that the Sacrament so celebrated is invalid when we reflect that in the third century it remained a grave question what the contents of the chalice should be, and that a man of St Cyprian's great authority could deem the use of wine alone to be equally reprehensible with the use of water alone.

was the proposal made by some who objected that it was disreputable that the smell of wine should be perceived about them in the morning. How does St Cyprian meet it? Certainly not as you would expect a modern casuist to meet it. He sets aside the objection as to the smell of wine in the morning, by saying that to be ashamed of this is to be ashamed of the blood of Christ; and if they fail to confess Christ in this, they will scarcely be ready to confess Him in martyrdom. He objects to the public celebration with water in the morning, and the private celebration with wine in the evening, simply on the ground that it would be impossible to call the people together to the domestic feast. He makes no objection to the double communion, or to the evening communion after the fast is broken—for the rule as to fasting now so rigorously insisted upon belongs altogether to a later date—but he justifies the morning as the proper time for a celebration, though Christ instituted the Sacrament in the evening, on this ground, namely: that it behoved Christ to offer at the evening of the day, for He was fulfilling the law of Exodus, which said: "The whole assembly of the congregation shall kill it in the evening." But (he added) we celebrate in the

Eucharist the Resurrection of the Lord, and as He rose in the morning we celebrate it in the morning.

The usage of private persons taking the Sacrament home with them to keep it in a casket or ark, continued more or less until the eighth century. Bingham says that it was the doctrine of transubstantiation which put an end to it. Certainly the practice had nothing in common with what is now meant by Reservation. Persons were allowed to take the Sacrament home and to treat it as they would, because it was *not* thought to be itself an object of worship. As soon as men believed in it as a locating of the Presence which they worshipped, it was treated with greater fear, and was no longer available for domestic rites. But still the family table is to be blessed, and God's good gifts are to be received with thanksgiving. Grace at every meal is the remembrance of the Eucharist, and of that which the Eucharist itself remembers.

If we take any large and comprehensive view of the Christian literature of the third century, we perceive that opinion was in a state of flux, or quite unformed upon many questions concerning the Holy Eucharist, upon which it has since become crystallized and sharply defined. Nevertheless, the Sacrament remains what it always was. Developments of doctrine which are really the unfolding of that which was from the beginning, are to be thankfully received, for they help us to a clear perception of what otherwise is but dimly seen. And we acknowledge it to be the special function of the Church, under the guidance of the Holy Spirit, thus to unfold the things of God to the growing intelligence of the ages. But accretions of doctrine which find no correspondence in the Scriptural revelation of the Master's purpose, and have no warrant in apostolic practice, must be discarded as superstitious—over and above and beyond that which God has been pleased to reveal.

To you and to me the Eucharist is the same thing that it was to St Paul or to Justin Martyr, or to St Cyprian. It was to them the pledge of a Christian profession; it implied participation in the altar of the Cross: it was the bond of unity in Christ. So it is to us, and so it ever must be to the faithful.

And the warning of the text is as pertinent

to-day as when St Paul wrote it, or as when Tertullian applied it and St Cyprian enforced it. Worldliness and sensuality are incompatible with allegiance to Christ. There is little need to urge people to Communion, for if they are fit for Communion they will desire Communion. But there is much need to warn them against coming unfitly, against making compromise with conscience, serving Mammon or Moloch or Baal in the week, and taking the oath of loyalty to Christ on Sunday. Whether St Cyprian's stories be true in fact or not, they are certainly true in moral. The child that is fed from the idol feast is unable to receive the chalice of Christ. The man who has defiled himself finds the Holy Bread turned to a cinder in his hand. The woman who would unworthily communicate is deterred by fire from her ark. "Ye cannot be partakers of the Lord's table and of the table of devils."

VIII.

THE EUCHARIST IN THE FOURTH CENTURY.

"Ask now of the days that are past."—*Deut.* iv. 32.

IN the last three sermons I have tried to set before you not indeed exhaustively, but fairly and typically, the testimony of the Christian literature of the first three centuries to the Eucharistic worship of the Church.

I have not selected passages favourable to any particular view of my own or of yours. I have wished to put you into possession of every significant note of primitive practice and doctrine with reference to the Blessed Sacrament in the writings of the period under review, so that you should be able to form your own estimate and conception of the mode in which the early Church presented to the faithful of those times the doctrine of the Holy Eucharist, and of the way in which the Holy Mysteries were regarded, and of the manner in which the very consecrated elements themselves were treated. Once in possession of the facts of history, you will draw your own inferences therefrom.

I have quoted from letters and treatises and lectures of the second and third centuries. I have not quoted from ancient liturgies; for though it is probable that such a liturgy as the Clementine contains much matter as old as the second century, yet liturgies were continually being re-edited, enriched, and enlarged, and this liturgy is only extant in the form which it had assumed in the latter half of the fourth century. It is only by comparing ancient liturgies together, and noting the features which are common to them all, that we arrive at any estimate of the original forms from which they were developed. For in the nature of the case a liturgy was not dealt with by editors as an epistle or a treatise would be dealt with. The latter were literary compositions, valuable in proportion to the authority and competency of their respective authors, and they would be copied and re-copied by successive generations without any substantial variation of their matter. But a liturgy was not valued as a literary composition, but as a handbook of worship, and as there was no desire in the early Church for a mechanical uniformity in worship, a liturgy would be continually subject to revision and improvement, each bishop seeking to enrich the use of his own diocese. Thus, for example, the prayer of St Chrysostom, which we use at the conclusion of morning and evening prayer, is the literal translation of a prayer found in the Greek Liturgy of St Chrysostom. But critics do not think it as old as that liturgy; it was probably an interpolation by which the liturgy was enriched at some unknown date.

Thus it is clear that historical arguments, based on isolated expressions in late editions of early liturgies, are very precarious, demanding much more caution and discrimination than inferences from any other form of literary composition.

But there has come down to us from the year 347 or 348, not a liturgy, but a course of catechetical lectures or instructions on the liturgy, which throw the clearest possible light on the public worship of the Church in the first half of the fourth century.

Just in the middle of the century, Cyril succeeded Maximus as bishop of Jerusalem. A few years previously he delivered the twenty-three lectures which we still possess. Eighteen of them were delivered in Lent in the basilica of the Holy Cross which Constantine had erected on the sacred site. These were addressed to candidates for baptism; the earlier ones are on a right disposition for baptism, and the rest constitute an exposition of the creed. The other five were delivered in Easter week, in the circular church of the Holy Sepulchre, built upon the traditional site of our Lord's burial, beyond the east end of the basilica. These five lectures were addressed to those who had been baptized on Easter Eve, and had received the unction and their first communion. The object of the instruction was to enlighten them upon the spiritual significance of the privileges to which they had been recently admitted. In the first of these Eastertide addresses Cyril recalls their renunciation of the devil and his works, and his pomp, and his service. In the second he describes the baptism itself, and in the third the anointing which had followed. He closes his course with two lectures, the one on the Real Presence and the other on the Communion Service.

His teaching on the Real Presence is very plain. He says: " Contemplate, therefore, the bread and wine, not as bare elements, for they are, according to the Lord's declaration, the Body and Blood of Christ. Judge not the matter from taste, but from faith be fully assured without misgiving that thou hast been vouchsafed the Body and Blood of Christ." And again: "Being fully persuaded that what seems bread is not bread, though bread by taste, but the Body of Christ. And that which seems wine is not wine, though the taste will have it so, but the Blood of Christ."

No words could be stronger than these to assert the presence of Christ in the mode in which He is pleased to communicate Himself to us.

Cyril uses the accustomed phraseology of the early Church. His words: "Contemplate the bread and wine not as bare elements," is almost an echo of Justin Martyr's language two hundred years earlier. "We do not receive them as ordinary food or ordinary drink, but . . . the food which was blessed by the prayer of the word which proceeded from Jesus, and from which our flesh and blood receive nourishment is (we are taught) both the flesh and blood of that Jesus who was made flesh."

It is, however, fair to notice that Cyril uses equally strong language concerning the presence in the water of baptism, and in the oil with which the baptized were anointed. Of the former he says: "Regard the sacred laver not as simple water ... for plain water after the invocation of the Holy Ghost and of Christ and of the Father, gains a sanctifying power," and of the chrism he says: "Beware of supposing this to be plain ointment; for as the Bread of the Eucharist, after the invocation of the Holy Ghost, is mere bread no longer but the Body of Christ, so also this holy ointment is no more simple ointment, nor (so to say) common, after the invocation, but the gift of Christ, and *by the presence of his Godhead it causes in us the Holy Ghost.*"

No one in these days would speak of a presence in the water of Baptism in terms equivalent to those by which churchmen of the Catholic school are accustomed to define the presence in Holy Communion. The real difference is sufficiently indicated when we point out that Baptism is held by the Church to be valid whether the water have been blessed or not, but that no Eucharist is valid without the consecration of the elements. But if we quote the early Church in regard to the Eucharistic presence, we are bound to remember that though they used language which would suggest even a natural and material presence in the consecrated elements, all that they meant was such a presence of Christ as could equally be predicated of the Holy Ghost in the water of Baptism or in the oil of chrism. And we may well reflect that the efficacy of the Blessed Sacrament to the communicant is dependent not on consubstantiation or transubstantiation, but on the word of Christ who spake it. If the presence were no more than that which we attribute to the water of Baptism, the Sacrament would still be to the communicant all that it is and all that it can be. Hooker puts this very strongly. After asserting that "the real presence of Christ's most blessed Body and Blood is not to be sought for in the Sacrament, but in the worthy receiver of the Sacrament," (and therefore, I suppose, in the worthy *receiving* of the Sacrament) he asks:

If on all sides it be confessed that the grace of baptism is poured into the soul of man, that by water we receive it, although it be neither seated in the water nor the water changed into it, what should induce men to think that the grace of the Eucharist must needs be in the Eucharist before it can be in us that receive it?

This is perhaps the most convenient point at which to discuss a question to which I am asked to give a clear and definite answer: namely, whether the literature of the first three hundred years of Christianity does or does not indicate a belief in the real objective presence of Christ in the Holy Sacrament.

I answer that no one can study this literature without being convinced that the Christians of these early days believed that in receiving the Sacrament they received a real objective grace; and that, in consequence of some actual potency present in the Sacrament itself. But the question how the Presence was to be regarded apart from the act of reception did not arise. For what is called non-communicating attendance had not yet been introduced, and Christians knew no other use to make of the Sacrament than to receive it according to the Lord's command. Sometimes, indeed, those who had privately reserved the Sacrament in their ark were tempted to ascribe some other virtue to it, as though it might be a charm against shipwreck or other temporal disaster. But such a use of the Sacrament, having no warrant in our Lord's institution, was regarded as superstitious (in the proper meaning of this word) and seems to have led to the subsequent rule forbidding the Sacrament to be carried away into private houses.

The use of the terms "subjective" and "objective" seem very puzzling to some; but we may say very simply that the benefit which we receive in Communion is subjective, if it be derived only from the exercise of our faith; it is objective if it be something conveyed to our souls from without us. It is subjective if it be our own effort; it is objective if it be God's gift. If it is subjective, we are doing something; if it is objective, God is doing something to us. There can be no doubt whatever about the mind of the early Church that in Communion the faithful receive an objective gift from God, conveyed to them in the consecrated bread and wine. But there was no need to speculate as to the conditions of the Presence apart from Communion, for, to the faithful, the Eucharist meant Communion, and the act of Eucharistic worship was the act of reception.

In his final lecture, Cyril sets vividly before us the celebration of the Eucharist as it was ordered in his day. He gives no account of what is sometimes called the ante-Communion service, for those whom he is instructing were sufficiently familiar with that. They had long been accustomed as catechumens and as competentes to join in the earlier part of the service. They were accustomed to hear the lesson from the prophets and the epistle and the gospel and the sermon; they were perhaps accustomed to join in the Creed, though some of the most ancient liturgies did not contain a creed. But then, all who were not going to receive were dismissed, first the catechumens and mere hearers, then the energumens, in whom the power of the Evil One was not yet subdued, then the competentes, or candidates for baptism, then those in penitence, who, though baptized, were for the time unworthy to receive. For long time those whom Cyril addresses had been dismissed with one or other of these classes, and had not witnessed the actual celebration of the mysteries. But since their baptism on Easter Eve they had been admitted to Communion, and Cyril explains to them the significance of the service in which they had taken part. I may abridge this part of his lecture as follows:

Ye saw the deacon give to the priest water to wash and to the presbyters, who stood round God's altar. He gave it not because of bodily defilement: no: for we did not set out for church with unclean bodies.

But this washing is a symbol that ye ought to be pure from all sinful and unlawful deeds: for since the hands are the symbol of action, by washing them we signify the purity of our conduct. Hast thou not heard the blessed David open this mystery, saying, "I will wash my hands in innocency, O Lord, and so will I go to thine altar?"

Then the deacon cries aloud, "Receive ye one another, and let us kiss one another." Think not that this kiss ranks with those given in public by common friends. This kiss blends souls one with another, and solicits entire forgiveness. The kiss is reconciliation, and therefore holy. As St Paul saith, "Greet ye one another with a holy kiss," and St Peter, "with a kiss of charity."

After this the priest cries aloud, "Lift up your hearts," bidding all in that hour abandon all worldly thoughts or household cares, to have their heart in heaven with the merciful God. Then ye answer, "We lift them up unto the Lord." But let no one come here who says with his lips, "We lift up our hearts unto the Lord," but in mind employs his thoughts on worldly business.

Then the priest says, "Let us give thanks unto the Lord," for in good sooth are we bound to give thanks that He has called us, unworthy as we are, to so great grace." Then ye say, "It is meet and right."

After this we make mention of all creation, rational and irrational, visible and invisible, of angels and archangels, and the seraphim who cried, "Holy, holy, holy, Lord God of hosts." We rehearse this confession of God delivered to us by the seraphim, that we may join in hymns with the companies of the world above.

Having sanctified ourselves by these spiritual hymns, we call upon the merciful God to send forth his Holy Spirit upon the gifts lying before Him, that He may make the bread the Body of Christ and the wine the Blood of Christ.

But at this point Cyril pauses. He gives no account of the consecration itself. Or, if he gave it orally, he abstains from writing it down. For the Christians of those times took the utmost care that the most sacred formulæ of their religion should not be made known to the unbelievers, lest they should treat holy things with any irreverence. But he continues:

After the spiritual sacrifice is perfected, the bloodless service upon that sacrifice of propitiation, we entreat God for the common peace of the Church, for the tranquillity of the world, for kings, for soldiers and allies, for the sick, for the afflicted—in a word, for all who stand in need of succour, we supplicate and offer this sacrifice.

Then we commemorate those also who have fallen asleep before us — patriarchs, prophets, apostles, martyrs—that at their intervention God would receive our petition. Afterwards for all who in past years have fallen asleep among us, believing that it will be an advantage to souls for whom supplication is put up while the holy and most awful sacrifice is presented.

After this we say the Lord's Prayer. Then the priest proclaims "Holy things to holy men." Then ye say, "One is holy, One is the Lord Jesus Christ." For truly One is holy, by nature holy. We too are holy, but not by nature, only by participation and discipline and prayer.

After this ye hear the chanter with a sacred melody inviting you to Communion, saying, "O taste and see that the Lord is good." Trust not the decision to thy bodily palate—no, but to faith unfaltering; for when we taste we are bidden to taste not bread and wine but the sign of the Body and Blood of Christ.

Approaching, therefore, make thy left hand a throne for thy right, which is on the eve of receiving the king: and having hallowed thy palm, receive the Body of Christ, saying after it Amen, giving heed lest thou lose any of it. For if any one gave thee gold dust, wouldest thou not with all precaution keep it fast? How much more cautiously then wilt thou observe that not a crumb falls from thee of that which is more precious than gold and precious stones.

Then, having partaken of the Body of Christ, approach to the Cup of his Blood, bending and saying in the way of worship and reverence, "Amen." Be thou hallowed by partaking also of the Blood of Christ. Then wait for the prayer, and give thanks unto God who hath accounted thee worthy of so great mysteries

Hold fast these traditions unspotted, and keep yourselves free from offence. Sever not yourselves from the Communion, deprive not yourselves by the pollutions of sins of these holy and spiritual mysteries. And the God of peace sanctify you wholly.[1]

From this brief summary of Cyril's last lecture you will perceive that the Liturgy of his time was substantially equivalent to the Communion Service of to-day. As time went on Liturgies were adapted to the conditions of different dioceses: they were enriched from time to time, or they were defaced by superstitious additions; but the substantial constitution of the service is still what it was more than fifteen centuries ago. For three hundred years after the resurrection the liturgical customs of the Church were in many respects unformed. We may take the great Nicene Council of 325 as sufficiently marking an epoch at which the Liturgy became crystallized in all its great and important features. It closes the period of the "Primitive Church." This is the appropriate point at which to pause in our historical studies.

If we try to sum up the results of our in-

---

[1] Abridged from the Oxford translation.

vestigations, we arrive at such conclusions as these.

The Holy Sacrament has always had its twofold virtue ; (1) as the means by which we claim participation in the great Atonement by eating of the sacrifice ; (2) as the means whereby our souls are strengthened and refreshed, as our bodies are naturally strengthened and refreshed by bread and wine. But in the earliest times the latter aspect appears to have been very little dwelt upon in comparison with the former.

Then we saw that in the first days every Christian received the Blessed Sacrament every Sunday, and those, at least, who were present at the service, received in both kinds. As time went on there appear to have been always some in penitence. It matters not whether they were under the penitential sentence of the Church, or accounted unworthy of Communion by the judgment of their own conscience. Cyril speaks of their depriving themselves of communion by their sins. They correspond to those who still have to excommunicate themselves at the tribunal of conscience, deeming themselves unfit for Communion. All these were sent out after the sermon, for it was a prevailing principle that those who were disqualified for Communion, were equally disqualified from joining in the great oblation.

Next, the passages which we have cited show this, that the service was at first essentially a thanksgiving, but that in process of time much more prominence was given to the idea of intercession. We find in Cyril this thought, that our intercessions will have a special efficacy if they be offered during the presentation of the Holy Sacrifice in which we are communicating. We have not yet come to the offering of masses for the living and the dead; but the germ of that later development is to be found in the gradual substitution of intercession in place of thanksgiving, as the great purpose of the celebration.

In Cyril also we have the first note of the later doctrine that the saints departed may intercede for us: that even our Communion will be more acceptable if the saints present our petition. This seems to have arisen from the exaggeration of the third century in attributing to martyrs a virtue which was allowed to supersede the discipline of the Church. Not only was baptism regarded as unnecessary in the case of martyrs, because their martyrdom was itself a baptism—that was a charitable view to take—but if one who was awaiting martyrdom wrote

The Eucharist in the Fourth Century.

on a scrap of paper a request that some under spiritual censure might be at once restored to Communion, the request was regarded as superseding the authority of bishop and priest. Whatever a martyr asked must be done. Cyprian complains that Church discipline was in this way completely subverted. From this position the transition was easy to the belief that the commemoration of martyrs in the Eucharist implied "that at their prayers and intervention God would receive our service."

Then we find that the early Church never hesitated to call the consecrated bread the Body of Christ, and the consecrated wine the Blood of Christ, though we may hesitate a little as to the meaning of this when we find almost parallel language used of the elements in baptism and unction. But Cyprian's stories of the portents attending attempts to communicate unfitly, and Cyril's comparison of the crumbs of the Sacrament with gold dust, show that they regarded the Sacrament as the most sacred thing in the world, in virtue of its supernatural qualities.

But throughout these early centuries no allusion can be found to the worship of Christ present in the Sacrament, in distinction from his presence universally with his Church. If anywhere, we should expect to find instruction on Eucharistic worship in Cyril's lectures. But though he fully explains the service, and uses unmistakable language as to the Real Presence, there is not the slightest hint of an object of worship present only when the Sacrament is present. But as the faithful, who were not disqualified by any sentence of penitential discipline, always communicated when the Sacrament was celebrated, and no others were allowed to assist, the question of modern times had not yet arisen, whether persons could worship Christ sacramentally, except by receiving. The Sacrament was carried away to private houses for the Communion of the absent, but there is no trace of its reservation in Church.

We found references in the third century to a domestic use of the Blessed Sacrament, and there seemed to be no rule then against persons communicating several times in the day. We infer from Cyril's lectures that no such abuse prevailed in his Church.

As to accessory ritual, we note that the Washing of the hands and the Kiss of Peace were in use in the fourth century. There is no trace of the ceremonial use of lights. As to incense, the early Christians associated it with heathen worship. Justin Martyr says expressly, "God has no need of sacrifices of blood, and libations, and incense," and Tertullian includes incense among the " foul things" which he describes the heathen as offering. He speaks of himself as the servant of God—

"Who alone give Him reverence, who offer to Him a sacrifice rich and dignified which He Himself hath commanded, the prayer that proceedeth from a chaste body, from a soul that sinneth not, from the Holy Spirit; not a penny-worth of incense; not the exudation of an Arabian tree; not two drops of wine; not the blood of a discarded beast; and after all these foul things a filthy conscience also."

As to vestments, the celebrant is spoken of in some early canons as endued with a shining garment. Naturally a man put on his best things for so sacred a function—and in time certain best things were reserved for the purpose. Ultimately certain appropriate forms would be evolved, in which ancient precedent would have much influence. There seems no ground for the assumption that vestments of the clergy are a survival either of heathen or of Jewish use.

The controversies of the day on these subjects are not very profitable; but if controversy be inevitable, it is well to enter it fully armed with knowledge. You ought at least to know what is primitive, what is mediæval, what is modern. You ought not to confuse that which was enjoined as to the use of the Sacrament with that which was tolerated when love grew cold. You ought to be able to distinguish local and temporary variations of use from that which satisfies the rule, *Quod semper, quod ubique, quod ab omnibus.*

The great thing is, that we use the Sacrament according to Christ's purpose and intention, (1) as the appointed way by which we claim participation in his great atonement, (2) as the means whereby we seek spiritual sustenance for our souls. Thus eating the Flesh of the Son of Man and drinking his Blood, we do show the Lord's Death till He come.

IX.

THE DIVINE OFFICE.

"Speaking to yourselves in psalms."—*Eph.* v. 19.
"Admonishing one another in psalms."—*Col.* iii. 16.
"Let him sing psalms."—*James*, v. 13.

IF we are asked what were the services of the Church in which the earliest Christians joined, we answer that there are traces of two such services, namely, the breaking of the bread and the singing of the psalms. And if we follow the practice of public worship through the ages, we find these two always prominent—the celebration of the Holy Eucharist, and the offices in which the psalms were sung.

The technical terms by which these two divisions of public worship were anciently distinguished were the Liturgy and the Divine Office. The Liturgy (or Divine Service) is the order of celebration and administration of the Holy Communion. The Divine Office is the arrangement by which the psalms are sung in the

Church, with the addition of such other devotions as have from time to time been associated with the Psalms.

Of the Liturgy we may speak on another occasion. My subject this morning is the Divine Office to which the Church calls her children, the office in which the Psalms anciently occupied so prominent a place, that we may consider the psalmody as the original thread on which the pearls of lesson, versicle, and collect were subsequently strung.

It may be said that, in the passages which I have quoted from St Paul and St James, the reference is to the use of the Psalms in private or in domestic worship, rather than in the great congregation. But it is certain from the frequent allusions of the earliest Christian writers, that there were public offices in which the Psalms were sung.

If the Last Supper, at which our Lord instituted the Holy Eucharist, partook of the nature of a family gathering, it was at the same time the assembly of the Church of Christ, and presented the prototype of all Christian worship. You will remember that on this occasion they sang a hymn: and if they followed, as they doubtless would, the prevailing custom of the

Passover, that hymn was the Hallel, consisting of six psalms, from the 113th to the 118th.

Ignatius, the disciple of St John the Evangelist, in his Epistle to the Ephesians, refers to the Christians singing in their worship. In Justin Martyr and Tertullian there are similar references. In some of these passages it is not expressly shown that what they sang were the Psalms of David, yet from what we know of the Jewish practice, and of our Lord's practice already cited, and of the custom which we presently find so fully developed in the Church, there is no doubt that the Psalms of David formed the staple of their singing.

Dr Neale has quoted from St Chrysostom a glowing passage on the use of the Psalms:

"If we keep vigil in the Church, David comes first, last, and midst. If early in the morning we seek for the melody of hymns, first, last, and midst is David again. If we are occupied with the funeral solemnities of the departed, or if virgins sit at home and spin, David is first, last, and midst. O marvellous wonder! Many who have made but little progress in literature, nay, have scarcely mastered its first principles, know the Psalter by heart. . . . In monasteries, among those holy choirs of angelic services, David is first, midst, and last. In the convents of virgins, where are the bands of them that imitate Mary; in the deserts, where are men crucified to this world, and having their conversation with God, first, midst, and last is David! Others sleep at night, but David is active: congregating the servants of God into seraphic bands he turns earth into heaven, and converts men into angels."

But the Psalms were said in old times with a zeal and perseverance unparalleled in the present day. Not only in monasteries, but in churches, the whole Psalter used to be recited every week, and there are many records of famous men who used to recite all the 150 psalms every day. St Patrick, the Apostle of Ireland, was one of these.

And if any one asks, how could the Psalms, which were written under the Old Testament, be regarded as suitable and almost in themselves sufficient for the devotion of Christians, the answer is plain. It is, that the Psalms are largely prophetic of Christ. In their temporal sense they may apply to David or to some other, but as David was a type of Christ and God's dealings with his chosen people were typical of his dealing with his Church, the temporal meaning of the psalm enshrines a spiritual and prophetic meaning, until almost every psalm is redolent of Christ. There was, indeed, sometimes a disposition to deny any temporal signification in the Psalms. Twice in his catechetical lectures Cyril insists that the psalms prophetic of Christ must not be interpreted of David or Solomon. We can hardly take this as a general rule, though it seems quite clear that some passages in the Psalms have a prophetic sense and no other: no other, at least, that is now intelligible to us. So St Peter insisted that David could not be speaking of himself, but only of Christ, when he said: "Thou wilt not leave my soul in hell, neither wilt thou suffer thine holy one to see corruption."

As I have said, the Psalms constituted the basis of the Divine Office, which was developed and completed by the addition of collects, versicles, and lessons; though the addition of lessons to the Divine Office does not seem to be so ancient as their introduction into the Liturgy, where they are known as the epistle and gospel. In course of time in the Western Church the saying of these psalms was distributed into seven portions, assigned to seven hours of the day.

Mattins and Lauds together made the chief morning office: Prime, Terce, Sext, and None were shorter and of less importance than the others. Vespers was distinguished by the recital of Magnificat, and Compline closed the day. In each office the Psalms occupied the principal place.

We can hardly avoid speaking of the Hours as separate offices, though, strictly speaking, they were said to constitute together the one Divine Office.

In our own Church of England the clergy were accustomed to say these offices daily until the new Prayer Book was introduced in 1549. In that book the Hours were rearranged in two offices, which were termed Mattins and Evensong; but Mattins and Evensong did not comprehend all that is now included in the order of Morning and Evening Prayer, but only the portion beginning with the Lord's Prayer and ending with the Third Collect. If you think of this by itself you will perceive what a prominent position the Psalms occupy in it.

And here let me say at once that the terms, "Order of Morning Prayer," and "Mattins," must not be treated as two names of the same thing. The term Mattins has never been applied by

The Divine Office.

authority to anything except the central portion. The order of Morning Prayer as it stands in the Prayer Book consists of three things:

I. A Preparation for Mattins (prefixed in 1552).
II. Mattins (arranged in 1549).
III. Supplementary Memorials and Intercessions (added in 1661);

and a precisely similar statement may be made with regard to Evensong and the order of Evening Prayer. The "preparation" prefixed in 1552 is entirely occupied with penitence. It begins with a sentence about repentance: then comes the Exhortation to Confession ; then the Confession itself, and the General Absolution. This preparation was, doubtless, introduced because the use of private confession and absolution was becoming less common ; and from 1552 to 1661 it was printed as part of the office. But in 1661, when Convocation drew up the book which is now in use among us, they seem to have been particularly anxious that the Penitential Preparation should not be regarded as an integral part of Mattins or Evensong. This, at least, is the only explanation of the fact that they drew a double line across the whole page in the order of both Morning and Evening Prayer, at the end of the Preparation; that is immediately after the Absolution and before the Lord's Prayer with which the office begins.[1]

In substituting Mattins and Evensong for the Seven Hours, the Reformers desired to put an end to certain abuses, and to remedy certain inconveniences.

And perhaps the chief abuse was this, that the Divine Office had come to be regarded as if it were intended for the clergy alone. This had not always been the case. St Paul was not addressing the clergy alone when he bid his converts speak to themselves in psalms, or admonish one another in psalms. St James had not a priest in mind when he wrote: "Let him sing psalms." There had been times when good laymen were even more eager for these offices than the clergy themselves. In a Constitution of the Emperor Justinian, the duty is pressed upon the clergy by the example of the laity. The edict runs thus: "If many laymen, resorting to church, are shewn to be assiduous in the

---

[1] This separation of the Penitential Preparation from Mattins and Evensong, though so marked in the manuscript Prayer Book of 1661, does not appear in the Prayer Book as usually printed. But the Convocation of Canterbury in 1879 recommmended its restoration

psalm-singing for their own soul's sake, how disgraceful would it be if clergy appointed for that very purpose, should not fulfil their office."

And Bede tells us of King Egbert, who made a vow that besides the psalmody in the canonical offices, in which, as a matter of course, he joined he would daily recite the whole Psalter.

The first care of the Reformers was to put the Divine Office into such a form as should suit the convenience of laymen as well as clergy, though its recital was still to be obligatory on the clergy only, and voluntary on the part of the laity. This was expressly set out in 1552, when it was ordered that though other priests and deacons might say the office, either privately or openly, the priest who had cure of souls must say it in the parish church, "and shall tolle a belle thereto a convenient tyme before he begyn that such as be disposed maye come to heare Goddes worde, and to praie with hym." And that all classes of people might the more readily take their part, the old Latin was abandoned, and the newly-arranged offices were put out entirely in English.

As the recital of the Psalms was the original basis of the Divine Office, we ought to notice first the change that was made in their recital. In the Hours certain psalms were said every week and certain others every day, whilst many were not recited at all. The Reformers retained only the Venite (in addition to the Canticles) to be said every day, but they arranged that the whole Psalter should be recited every month. It was by thus avoiding the daily repetition of a large number of psalms that the total length of the office was curtailed, and the Seven Hours reduced to two offices.

Another alteration which they made was in the introduction of whole chapters of the Bible, so that in the course of the year all the more important books of the Old Testament were read through, whilst the New Testament, with the exception of the Book of Revelation, was read through three times.

But the characteristic features of the old office were carefully preserved. We are, therefore, to regard our present Mattins and Evensong as the lineal representative to us of the ancient offices in which Christians throughout the ages have loved to sing the Psalms of David. Those who in apostolic days came together on the first day of the week to break bread, came together at other times to speak to one another in psalms and hymns and spiritual songs. And ever since, the Church has broken the bread according to the Liturgy and sung the psalms according to the Divine Office. Ever since, as now in our own Church, not only is the daily Eucharist celebrated, but the daily psalms are said. Mattins and Evensong are provided by Catholic rule as well as the Christian Sacrifice.

Thirty years ago a demand was loudly made for shortened services. Clergy who did not hesitate to leave the daily offices entirely unsaid, had a scruple against omitting only a part of the order. They thought, for instance, that if they said Mattins and Evensong they were bound to say the Preparations before each office and the whole of the Supplementary Memorials at the end. To relieve the consciences of these brethren Convocation enacted a canon, which was accepted by the State in the Act of Uniformity Amendment Act of 1872, declaring that on a weekday the Preparation might be shortened by the omission of the Exhortation to Confession, and the Supplementary Memorials might be omitted altogether. To our great regret they also authorized some mutilation of Mattins and Evensong themselves; but as the enactment is only permissive, no well-instructed churchman avails himself of the liberty thus given him. No one, for instance, who knows that the Divine Office is but the developed method of reciting the Psalter, would wish to omit some of the psalms for the day and leave them unsaid for the month. And no one who values the Holy Scriptures would wish to omit either of the lessons. If the exhortation to Confession is omitted, and the Memorials after the office, none can say that the office is too long even for the hurry and impatience of the present day.

But I am told of some who prefer to recite the Divine Office in the form of the Hours according to the Pre-Reformation use. Well, if they be lay-people, they are under no obligation to use the present form, and if they think it better to say certain psalms every day of the year, and certain others every week, while more than half are left unsaid (and amongst these that most beautiful Psalm, the 103rd)—if they think this better than to follow the Church's use and recite the whole Psalter every month, no one may condemn them. But if they think that it is more Catholic (as they say) to recite the Hours, then they are grievously mistaken, unless indeed they wish to renounce altogether the

English Church, or to decry its claim to be Catholic. For that revision of the Divine Office which was effected in 1549 was canonically made, and it has been delivered to us with all spiritual authority by the Convocation of our Church in 1661. By every Catholic principle, unless indeed our Church be no Church, Mattins and Evensong form for us the Divine Office to which the clergy are bound and to which the laity are called by the voice of Holy Church.

The old offices were specially designed to meet the necessities of people of whom very few could read. It was thought that by repeating the same psalms day after day the congregation would soon know them by rote. In fact, in ancient times, books were little used even by the clergy, and it was ruled by the second Council of Nicæa that no one might be made a bishop unless he knew the Psalter by heart. Pope Gregory the Great refused to advance one Rusticus a deacon, saying, " He is a vigilant man indeed, but, according to report, he does not know the psalms."

In the English Reformation there was a deliberate purpose to encourage reading. This was explained in the preface to the Prayer-Book of 1549, when it was said:

If any would judge this way more painful because that all things must be read upon the book, whereas before by the reason of so often repetition they could say many things by heart: if those men will weigh their labour with the profit in knowledge which daily they shall obtain by reading upon the book, they will not refuse the pain in consideration of the great profit that shall ensue thereof.

This quaint apology for the use of a Prayer-Book remained in the preface until the revision of 1661.

But among the restorations effected in the Divine Office at the time of the Reformation, we ought to be especially thankful for the place given to the reading of Holy Scripture. I am afraid that while the blessings of education are now being widely extended the people are not advancing at the same rate in their knowledge of the word of God. I am afraid for you, sirs, that while you are much better read than your grandfathers were in science and philosophy, you do not know your Bibles as well as they did. The lessons in church must be treated with the greatest dignity, read with the utmost care, and listened to with strained attention.

The Divine Office.

The effect of the Reformation upon the Divine Office may therefore be stated in five points.

I. The language was changed from Latin to English.

II. The Seven Hours were rearranged as two offices.

III. The people were called to assist in what had come to be regarded as the concern of the clergy only.

IV. The recitation of the Psalms was rearranged in harmony with ancient precedent.

V. An important place was given to the reading of Holy Scripture.

Independently of this revision of the office itself, certain other steps have been subsequently taken. The Penitential Preparation was prefixed in 1552, and the Supplementary Memorials were added in 1661. In 1871 the table of lessons was revised, and in 1872 the permissive canon for shortened services was enacted.

People sometimes speak of our incomparable Liturgy. If they use the word Liturgy in its proper sense as denoting the order of Holy Communion, some will dispute the justice of the epithet "incomparable." Some, for instance, think that the Scottish Liturgy is to be preferred above the English. But if they are speaking of the Divine Office of Mattins and Evensong, I think they are justified in calling it incomparable. There is no office of any church, ancient or modern, worthy to be compared with it, whether we apply the test of conformity to ancient precedent or the test of the fulness of scriptural teaching, whether we judge it by the intelligent part that is given to the congregation, or by its fervent expression of faith and praise, or by its general tendency to edification.

Therefore, my people, you will take every opportunity of assisting at the Divine Office on a weekday as well as on a Sunday. Your highest act of worship is indeed to be found not in this office but in your communion. But in the Divine Office you fulfil the apostolic precept to speak to yourselves in psalms: and you do this not according to any private judgment, but at the bidding of your Holy Mother Church.

But there are many who cannot be present at the daily offices of the Church. Let me urge upon them that in their private prayers they should not forget the ancient custom of reciting psalms. Private prayers are apt to be much relaxed if their necessity be measured only by the urgency of petition. There are times when we feel that we hardly want to ask any special thing of God—we want simply to rest upon his will. But praise is always in season. So it is always fitting that David be "first and last and midst."

Or to put it otherwise, praise is easier than petition. We often know not for what we should ask, but God in his person and attributes is ever worthy of our praise.

And perhaps the nearer we approach the heavenly throne the more do our prayers merge themselves in praise. The hour of petition may be past: it may remain to the resigned soul only to pray, "Thy will be done." But it is never too late to take up David's words, and say, "Praise the Lord, O my soul: and all that is within me praise his holy name."

X.

THE LITURGY.

"This do in remembrance of me."—*St Luke*, xxii. 19.

WE inquired, last Sunday, what was the worship in which from the beginning Christians joined in their public assemblies. We found that they came together for the Breaking of the Bread, and for the singing of the Psalms— for the two sacred actions which were subsequently known as the Divine Service or Liturgy, and the Divine Office.

We traced the Divine Office through the centuries. We saw that the prominent feature in it was always the reciting of the Psalms: that the Psalms were (as some one said) the thread on which were strung the pearls of collect, canticle, and lesson. We noted that the Divine Office was arranged in mediæval times as seven hours, and that at the Reformation these seven hours were reduced to two offices, Mattins and Evensong, and that at the same time the Church guarded against the error of its being supposed that these offices were for the clergy only. She called all her children to them. We thus found that Mattins and Evensong, as we say them now, are the development in direct succession of the office in which the Christian Church of every age has loved to say the Psalms.

As we studied the Divine Office last Sunday, let us this morning study the Liturgy or Communion service.

I have already called your attention to some of the most interesting writings which have come down to us from the fourth century, the Catechetical lectures of Cyril of Jerusalem, which he delivered as a priest in the year A.D. 347 or 348, to those of his flock who had recently been admitted to the holy mysteries. You will remember that in the last of these lectures he gives an outline of the celebration of Holy Communion as it took place fifteen and a half centuries ago. But he only begins at the point at which the uninitiated were dismissed. He says nothing therefore about the epistle, or gospel, the creed, or the sermon. Those whom he addressed had been accustomed to be present at what is now called the ante-communion service, and they knew all about it. He begins with the priest's ablution and the kiss of peace. Then he tells his children how the priest cries aloud, "Lift up your hearts," and ye answered, "We lift them up unto the Lord:" that then the priest says, "Let us give thanks unto the Lord," and ye say, "It is meet and right." After this (he continues) we make mention of heaven and earth, of angels and archangels—of the seraphim whom Esaias by the Holy Ghost beheld, who cried, "Holy, Holy, Holy, Lord God of Hosts." Then he mentions the prayer which is still found in all Eastern liturgies, that God will send the Holy Ghost upon the elements to make the bread the Body of Christ, and the wine the Blood of Christ. This invocation of the Holy Ghost is neither in the Roman nor the Sarum Missal, but our learned Reformers introduced it into the first Prayer Book of Edward VI., though it was dropped in the next book. It is, however, retained in the Scottish and American liturgies. Where it is absent it is not through any defect of doctrine. For the operation of the Holy Ghost is of course equally implied in the Prayer of Consecration which immediately follows.

Cyril then speaks of the great Prayer of Intercession for the living, and commemoration of the departed, completed with the Lord's

Prayer, which he expounds. After this (he tells us) the priest says "Holy things to holy men," and ye respond, "One is holy, one is the Lord Jesus Christ," and the chanter says, "O taste and see that the Lord is good." Then follows the communion of the people, and the service is closed by prayer and thanksgiving.

We pass on for twelve hundred years, and come to our own country, and we find the Communion Service still corresponding in most of its prominent features to the description given by Cyril.

If we turn to the Sarum Missal in use in our English Church immediately before the Reformation, we find after the Creed the priest's ablution; the Sursum Corda: "Let us give thanks," with its answer, "It is meet and right": the association of the worshippers with all the company of heaven: the seraphic Sanctus: the great Prayer of Intercession for the living, and Memorial of the departed, in which the Prayer of Consecration is set: then the kiss of peace and the priest's Communion. All these are notes of identity between the liturgies of the fourth and of the sixteenth centuries. But there is one sad deficiency in the Sarum Missal. Cyril in the fourth century had taught his children to receive the Sacrament, "the Body of Christ," and "the Cup of his Blood," but in the Missal of the sixteenth century no provision whatever is made for the Communion of the people. It is thought that some of them did occasionally receive after the priest, though there is no rubric to indicate this. More often, perhaps, they made their communion as we have sometimes witnessed it in papal countries, quite apart from the Divine Service. But at least we gather this, that Communion had become so rare that it was quite exceptional to have any lay people to communicate at a celebration: the normal condition was that the priest alone received. As far as the people were concerned Christ's command to "Take, eat," was altogether separated from "Do this." It was this departure from Christ's institution that the Reformers set themselves first to remedy.

I speak of the action of the Reformers without staying at this point to distinguish between the influence of Church and State in the work of reformation, or to investigate the canonical authority of the earlier prayer books. For the spiritual authority of our present Prayer Book does not in the least depend upon the spiritual authority of the books issued in 1548, 1549, 1552, or 1558. It must never be forgotten that the present

Prayer Book was drawn up and adopted by the Convocations of the Church in 1661, and that on every Catholic principle its authority was complete—complete in itself without any reference to previous editions of the book.[1]

[1] The English Liturgy was recently disparaged by a popular preacher as "a parliamentary Communion service"; but in fact, though the Prayer Book has the sanction of both Church and State, it was drawn up entirely by the Convocation of the Church, and so far from being a Parliamentary book, it was actually adopted to the exclusion of a rival book composed under the auspices of the House of Commons. We have only to go back to the Restoration of the Monarchy in 1660. The use of the old prayers had been made penal by Act of the Republican Parliament, and it seemed to some that the authority of Parliament would now be sufficient to put forth a new Prayer Book. On May 11, 1661, the House of Commons appointed all their members learned in the law to be "a Committee for Religion," and on July 9 a Bill for Uniformity was read a third time, and sent up to the Lords, with a book attached to it which may, undoubtedly, be properly described as a Parliamentary Prayer Book. But it was quickly perceived that no true churchman would submit to such a violation of the Reformation settlement as to accept a Prayer Book drawn up by the lawyers of the House of Commons, and propounded with the sole authority of the State without the Church. Letters of business were granted to the Convocations of Canterbury and York, and they set to work to produce a revision of the old Prayer Book in competition with the proposed Parliamentary book. Their labours were concluded on December 20, 1661, when the

Nevertheless, the evolution of the present Liturgy from that which existed before the Reformation is a matter of interest to all loyal churchmen, and to this I call your attention.

The first care of the Reformers was to make the communion of the people an integral part of the service, and to establish it as communion in both species. With this view, in 1548 they added at the end of the Latin mass an English supplement consisting of an office of Preparation of the communicants followed by the formula of

new book was subscribed by the Bishops and Clergy of both Convocations. This book was brought into the House of Lords, attached to a Bill of Uniformity, on February 25, 1662. Thus the Lords had before them two proposed Prayer Books, viz., the Parliamentary book, and the Convocation book. Of course, there were many who wished that the Parliamentary Prayer Book should be adopted; and early in the session pressure seems to have been put upon the Lords not to wait for the Bishops' book. It was a critical hour for the Church of England; but under the providence of God the wiser counsels prevailed. The Upper House rejected the Parliamentary Prayer Book, and accepted that which the Convocations had adopted. The Bill of Uniformity with the Prayer Book annexed was afterwards passed by the Commons, and received the Royal Assent on May 19, 1662. The new Prayer Book came into use on St Bartholomew's Day, the Thirteenth Sunday after Trinity, 1662, and it has remained in use ever since, "the most popular Service-book in Christendom."

communion in both kinds. This English supplement to the Latin Liturgy is of great interest: firstly, for its own inherent value; secondly, because there was nothing quite like it in ancient liturgies, where the Preparatory office was restricted to the priest and his assistants; thirdly, because all its parts have remained ever since, slightly revised and transposed, to the great enrichment of the English office; and fourthly, because with the exception of an alternative warning to those who neglect Communion, and perhaps four or five lines besides, no other new matter has been at any subsequent epoch introduced into the English Liturgy.

The supplement began with the "Warning" to the parishioners that they prepare themselves for the Communion—very much as it now stands in the Book of Common Prayer. Then there came that instructive and beautiful address to those that mind to come to the Holy Communion, which under present arrangements is not heard as often as we should desire. This concluded with a passage (now incorporated in the Warning) calling upon the blasphemer, adulterer, or other grievous sinner not to come to the Holy Table till he have yet awhile bewailed his sins. And the priest was ordered to "pause awhile to see if any man will withdraw himself: and if he perceive any so to do, then let him commune with him privily at convenient leisure and see whether he can with good exhortation bring him to grace." After a little pause the priest was to say the short exhortation, "Ye that do truly and earnestly repent"; then followed the Confession, the Absolution, the Comfortable Words, and the Prayer of Humble Access, as we have them at present in the Prayer Book; and then the people were communicated, first from the paten and then from the chalice.

Meanwhile Convocation was engaged in the revision of the Latin mass. That it should be henceforth said in the vernacular instead of an unknown tongue was itself a return to primitive usage. But some other points needed attention. It was not very appropriate to claim communion with such obscure saints as are found in the list of "Linus, Cletus, Clement, Sixtus, Cornelius, Cyprian, Laurence, Chrysogonus, John and Paul, Cosmos and Damian," or to ask fellowship with "Ignatius, Alexander, Marcellinus, Felicitas, Perpetua, Agatha, Lucy, Agnes, Cecilia, and Anastasia," with many of whom the people must have been practically unacquainted. These lists of names were omitted. Further, the prayers to be said secretly by the priest were found to contain expressions which seemed to imply (though they were not intended to imply) a material rather than a real and sacramental presence in the elements. These were revised; and in general all prayers which had been said secretly by the priest were so rearranged that the people might have part in them. The new preparation of the communicants was retained; but as the preparation proper for the people must be proper also for the priest, the celebrant's own communion was deferred until after the preparation had been said. Some of the ceremonies of the mass were reduced; as, for instance, when it was ordered that the consecration should be made without any elevation or showing of the Sacrament to the people. The kiss of peace was omitted, but the invocation of the Holy Ghost on the elements was introduced from ancient liturgies. Thus was the first Liturgy of Edward VI. constructed in a spirit conservative of Catholic practice, but decisive for the reform of all that was unedifying or corrupt. Yet the book was very far from perfect. From one point of view it might be said to be less true to Catholic precedent than any other liturgy of the Church of England; and yet it is the liturgy which some churchmen desire to see restored—or at least allowed as an alternative to our present order.

It had been a step in the right direction when, in 1548, the English Communion of the people was added on at the end of the Latin mass. The offering of the sacrifice and the reception of the sacrament were thus brought into one service; but they were still apart: one was finished before the other began. This unsatisfactory feature remains in the first Prayer Book of Edward VI., and it is even aggravated by the celebrant's own communion being deferred until after the preparation of the communicants. The Consecration was made, the Canon was concluded; then began the preparation of the communicants; after that, the priest received, and last of all the people. Christ said, "take eat" in one breath with "do this," and the communion of the priest has always been associated very closely with the act of consecration. The much-vaunted Liturgy of 1549 affords the one notable exception to this rule.

I am sure we are to be thankful for the rearrangement of the service which was made in 1552, and confirmed in 1558 and 1661. Two of the changes then made have been much criticised, and I allow that they are fairly open to criticism. Fairly and honestly we may be divided in our opinion as to whether these two changes were improvements or not. One was that the Gloria in Excelsis was moved from the beginning to the end of the service, giving to our English service (as many have maintained) a more glorious conclusion than any other Liturgy in Christendom can show. The other was that the great prayer of intercession and oblation in which the Consecration was formerly set, was broken up into three parts, known now as the Prayer for the Church Militant, the Prayer of Consecration, and the Prayer of Self Oblation. Whatever may be thought of these changes no one who regards either Catholic use or present edification can fail to thank God for the re-arrangement by which the preparation of the communicants no longer intervenes between the Consecration and the Communion, but is made the fitting approach to the solemnity of the Consecration itself.

And here I think a great spiritual principle is enforced. It seems to be sometimes thought that persons may be fit to join in offering the Eucharistic sacrifice though they are not fit to communicate. Waiving for the moment the question whether there is any way of joining in the offering except by eating of the sacrifice, it is quite clear, as the teaching of Holy Scripture and of the early Church, that spiritual fitness is required before we can make an acceptable oblation. The offering of the wicked is an abomination in the sight of the Lord, and the prayer of the impious man is turned into sin. So the same ecclesiastical censure which excluded a man from communion forbad him also to take part in the oblation. Wisely, therefore, did our Church transfer the preparation of the communicant to the earlier part of the service, that his heart might be ready for the sacrifice itself.

We frequently hear it asserted that the Reformers robbed the Liturgy of an important feature by the omission of the priest's preparation. Thus an author, generally most trustworthy, whose "History of the Church of England" is in the hands of many of you, and is highly esteemed by all who know it, says of the compilers of the book of 1549: "They omitted almost entirely the preparation of the priest both before he began mass and before be began the canon."[1] And again: "The omission

[1] Wakeman's "Introduction to the History of the Church of England," 5th edit., p. 276.

of the priest's preparation and some of the ceremonies at mass, seems to be founded on no reason at all, and be simply due to haste or carelessness."[1] But, in fact, the Reformers here acted upon the great principle which guided them throughout their work, that much which had hitherto been restricted to the clergy, should now be made available for the whole congregation. They did not omit the priest's preparation, but they so recast it, that it should henceforth be the preparation of priest and people together. In the Sarum missal the preparation, which we are said to have lost, was confined to the priest and his ministers, as if they alone were the performers of the service; in our present Liturgy the preparation occupies much more space, and all the worshippers join in it. So far from the element of preparation being absent from our service, it is much more prominent than in any previous Liturgy. The preparation begins with the collect for purity, once said secretly by the priest in his private devotions, now said aloud that the whole congregation may add their *Amen*. Then comes the recitation of God's Law, that all may recall

[1] Wakeman's "Introduction to the History of the Church of England," 5th edit., p. 279.

their offences, and ask of God mercy and grace. Further on we have the confession and absolution, and the comfortable words, and the prayer of humble access, all of which are intended to dispose priest and people alike for the great action in which they are to engage, a preparation not for communion only (as it might have seemed in 1548 and 1549), but for the great act of Eucharistic worship, as the present arrangement of the service testifies.

I have now indicated the changes through which our Liturgy has passed from the earliest times to the present day. From what I have suggested you will draw the sound inference that never, either at the Reformation period or any other, was any such radical change effected as would justify the common and ignorant judgment that at some epoch the mass was abolished and the communion service substituted for it. It is one and the same sacrament, whether it be called the Mass or the Lord's Supper or the Holy Communion or the Holy Eucharist. The change of the Name is not a change in the thing, though it may imply a change in the point of view from which the thing is regarded. There was no point at which it could be said that one thing was abolished and another adopted in its place, unless indeed the change of language from Latin to English could be thus described; yet in English Prayer Books of 1549, the Holy Communion was still said to be "commonly called the Mass." In later times this name has been discarded, and wisely. For though it has no inherent significance to which objection could be made, yet it has become irrevocably associated with an aspect of the Sacrament in which the action of the priest is everything, and the communion of the people is of little account. As long as the term "hearing mass" is used in contradistinction to "receiving communion," no well-instructed catholic will willingly accept "mass" as a suitable designation of the Sacrament; for the usage excludes the fundamental truth that by eating the Flesh of the Son of Man and drinking His Blood, we do show the Lord's death till He come.

It will have been observed that our Liturgy of the present day contains every feature described by Cyril fifteen and a half centuries ago, with the exception of the ceremonial washing of the hands, the kiss of peace, the invocation of the Holy Ghost, and the proclamation, "Holy things for holy men." But not one of these is of such a character that its omission can be said to indicate a radical change of rite. The invocation of the Holy Ghost is certainly the most important of these; and it is wanting in the Roman rite as well as in our own.

The true statement of the case is this, that the Church of England as a living church has in her own inherent right from time to time revised her Liturgy to the greater edifying of her children: she has translated and transposed: she has eliminated mediæval expressions of doubtful doctrine: she has omitted allusions which in course of time had lost their significance: she has restored catholic features which had been overlaid by the corruptions of time: but she has never tampered with the essential and characteristic elements of the service, handed down from primitive times, and generally accepted in the Church.

It is a glorious action and one of spiritual exhilaration when we join in one unchanged and unchangeable service with the Church of every Christian century: when we break the bread as the apostles broke it, and bless the cup as the apostles blessed it: when we say the Sursum Corda, and sing the Seraphic Song as Cyril taught them to his spiritual children : when we show the Lord's death as St Augustine and St Chrysostom showed it; as Augustine of Canterbury showed it, and Anselm and Thomas à Becket, and Fisher of Rochester, and Archbishop Laud, yea, and as all the faithful laity in the Church through all these ages showed it—as many as obeyed the Divine command and followed the apostolic precept, sealing the covenant in the Eucharistic feast.

But we do this not in the capacity of private individuals but as members of the Church of England. The claim which some make to be Christians at large, or priests at large, subject to no immediate ecclesiastical authority, is unwarranted in the Catholic Church. As churchmen we must obey those that have the rule over us, and submit ourselves. In the Church of England, we can only minister by the authority of the Church, and under the terms in which she has commissioned us. If we substitute for her order some other rule or rite, however ancient, however catholic, we are acting outside our commission, our action is lawless and therefore uncatholic, and we can look for no grace in what we do.

If the Church of England be not a living branch of the Catholic Church, we have no business here. Our very baptism is irregular and the ordination of our priests is invalid.

If the Church of England be not Catholic, we have certainly received no Catholic rite except our baptism. We may share with baptized nonconformists a certain membership in the Catholic Church, because baptism, though irregular or even heretical, may yet be valid. But if we claim to be Catholics in any other sense than this, it must be through some inherent virtue of Catholicity which belongs to the Church of England. Only by the agency of the Church of England have our clergy received Holy Orders; only by the ministry of bishops and priests of the Church of England have we received Confirmation and Communion. If our Mother Church be base-born, it is vain for her sons to boast of their legitimacy. We are Catholics because the Church of England is Catholic.

But if the Church of England be a living branch of the Catholic Church, then she is that to which we owe allegiance. She is the presentment to us of the Catholic Church; and the Prayer Book, being the voice of the Church of England, is therefore to us the voice of the Catholic Church; and disobedience to the

Prayer Book is the rejection of Catholic authority.

If the Church of England be not a living branch of the Church we must leave her; but if she be, then as Catholics we must obey her.

NOTE.

APPRECIATION OF THE BOOK OF COMMON PRAYER.

The following address, delivered at the Diocesan Conference at Bangor in 1898, will suitably follow here, though it involves some slight repetition of statements already made in the sermons.

SUBJECT.—"The importance of making the Prayer Book of the Church of England the rule of conduct, devotional and practical, in the lives of its members."

A Book of Common Prayer was practically impossible when few could read, and no mechanical means were known to supply even these few with books.

In the early days of Christianity the possession of a copy of the Gospels was a luxury which only the wealthiest individuals could enjoy. The church might possess a treasured manuscript of the Holy Scriptures for use in the congregation, but for a private person able to read, a small collection of "Sayings of Jesus" would suffice; while the majority of the people could make no use of a book. But from apostolic times Christians were accustomed to come together to break the Bread and to sing the Psalms. No doubt at first the sacred story of our Lord's institution of the Holy Eucharist was recited at the celebration from memory; but very soon manuscripts of the Liturgy were edited for the use of the clergy, the principal features of our present communion service having been clearly established and become practically stereotyped before the fourth century. As to the other act of worship, the psalms remained the golden cord on which were strung the pearls of collect and versicle and lesson. In the Middle Ages the saying of the Psalms was arranged in seven offices known as the Hours, and at the Reformation these were rearranged as two offices of Mattins and Evensong. Our present Prayer Book, as you know full well, includes in its provision for daily devotion each of the two primitive forms of worship. (1) There is the Breaking of the Bread—the Liturgy or Communion Service, and (2) there is the Psalter, with its rich setting in the order of Morning and Evening Prayer.

The great reform which made the old Service Books of the Church of England into a veritable Book of Common Prayer, was effected in the sixteenth century, when the offices and prayers which had been provided for the clergy were adapted to the use of the faithful in general. It had come to be thought that the Divine Office of the Hours concerned the clergy alone, but when these Hours were rearranged as Mattins and Evensong, the parish priest was directed to say them daily, not by himself; but to cause a bell to be tolled a convenient time beforehand, that the people also might come and hear God's word and pray with him. Thus you have the mind of the Church clearly expressed as to your attendance at Mattins and Evensong.

And as regards the Liturgy the priest was no longer to make a solitary communion; but the communion of the people was to become a prominent element in the service. In the old liturgies forms had been given for the personal preparation of the priest. These forms of preparation were not now relegated, as some seem to think, to the vestry, to be used privately by the priest, but on the contrary they were re-cast and made an integral part of the Liturgy, so that priest and people might prepare together for participation in the Holy Mystery. We ought to be thankful indeed for the possession of a Prayer Book which treats priest and people alike in their personal right of access to the throne of grace, recognizing the equal need of each to be fed with the bread of life, recognizing the qualification of all to worship in the Body of Christ.

We have no misgivings—we make no reservation—in committing ourselves to the acceptance of the Book of Common Prayer as our ample and sufficient guide in Public Worship.

Nor ought its merits to be overlooked as a manual of private prayer. Doubtless there are petitions and intercessions and thanksgivings which we must offer to God in our own words, and no manual whatever can supersede the necessity of this freedom in our private devotion. But when we desire to make an act of worship before God—solemn and dignified, and expressive of our due attitude before Him—an act of worship that shall lift us up and build us up in our most holy faith—that shall be at once for God's glory and for our own comfort and edification, I do not think that we can more worthily occupy fifteen or twenty minutes than by using, even in private, the Office of Mattins or Evensong. Of course, the clergy are bound to say these offices in private if not in public; but though the recitation of them be not enjoined on the laity as an obligatory duty, yet priest and people are of one human nature, alike in their spiritual needs: what is good for priest is good for people.[1] The daily use of Mattins and Evensong would at least correct some of the common faults of private prayer, in which petition and intercession are apt to occupy too much space to the neglect of thanksgiving and to the exclusion of praise.

But the Prayer Book is to us much more than a directory of worship, public or private. It gives us in the Catechism a manual of faith and duty; it asserts by the occasional offices the claims of God and Holy Church at every epoch of our lives; whilst

---

[1] In speaking of the daily office I do not necessarily include the preparatory office of penitence, and the supplemental commemorations which have been more lately joined to Mattins and Evensong to make up the order of Morning and Evening Prayer.

the book from cover to cover is full of incidental teaching, as to doctrine and practice.

The child is taught from the beginning that it is not a child of wrath, the fair denizen of hell, lost for ever, unless by some miracle of conversion hereafter its destiny be changed. The child has been brought to God in Holy Baptism; he is taught to think of himself as a member of Christ, a child of God, one who has received an inheritance in God's kingdom of grace. He is taught to thank God that he has been called to this state of salvation; he is taught to pray that he may continue in the same. He is not in a city of wrath from which he must flee, but in the Jerusalem of grace from which he must take care not to fall.

Parents, it surely makes all the difference in the world to the happiness of the child on whom the consciousness of God is just dawning—that he is not to think of himself as in daily danger of hell—but as being already in the grace and love of God, in a position in which he must pray to God to keep him—from which he must take heed not by any wilful sin to fall away.

But the Church refuses to deal with the child as if he were a full-grown man. She calls for sponsors to put him in mind of his sacred responsibilities. She calls upon "all fathers, mothers, masters, and dames" to cause their "children, servants, and apprentices" to come to church to be instructed in the faith. She enjoins upon the children that they submit themselves to their governors, teachers, spiritual pastors, and masters, and that they order themselves lowly and reverently to all their betters.

And when the child comes to years of discretion, when temptations are multiplied, and the powers of the devil, and the world, and the flesh seem to be terribly intensified, then he is taught to look to God for more grace, greater grace in greater danger, greater grace to sustain greater responsibility, new measures if not new kinds of grace to meet the new conditions of maturer life, the seven-fold gifts of the Holy Ghost bestowed in Confirmation.

And he is taught to look upon the life before him as the vocation to which God calls him. He cannot choose for himself the path that he shall tread; he must run the race that is set before him; or if there be some scope for choice, that choice is to be exercised with a solemn sense of God's over-ruling providence, while he listens for the voice of divine guidance. From very infancy he is taught that he must do his duty in that state of life to which it shall please God to call him.

It has already been implied that the faithful Christian will live his life in the strength of habitual communion. As often as the Sacrifice of Calvary is pleaded upon the altar, the spiritual banquet is spread, and the faithful are called to participate in it. This is at once the sacramental strengthening and refreshing of their souls, and the mode whereby they join in the great action by which they show the Lord's death till He come.

But the churchman is not to take his part in the

great oblation in any perfunctory manner, nor without regard to his spiritual fitness. For the sacrifice of the wicked is an abomination in the sight of the Lord, now as it was in Old Testament times.

The Prayer Book is most emphatic in its teaching that we must approach the altar with the full assurance that all our sins are forgiven, and that we are for the time being in the grace of God. This doctrine of assurance of present salvation must not be confounded with the doctrine of the "insurance" of our eternal life which is nowhere found in the Prayer Book—the doctrine, I mean, that if we have once accepted the gospel call we cannot possibly fall away to eternal perdition. He that thinketh he standeth must ever take heed lest he fall. But the Church is quite clear in expecting and requiring that the faithful member of Christ should approach the holy mysteries with a quiet conscience, not saying that he has not sinned, but knowing that his sins are forgiven.

And on the subject of sin the Church speaks with no uncertain sound. Witness the teaching of the Commination Service. The vulgar and thoughtless disparage that service as though we were cursing our neighbours therein. We do not invoke a curse on any one, but we acknowledge the fact of the curse of sin. We do not say "cursed be he," but "cursed is he." And the person whom we have in mind when we thus confess the deathliness of sin is not our neighbour but ourself. The commination is the recognition of the doom of God's righteous wrath upon ourselves unless we repent. We say *Amen*, not praying that it may be so, but assenting to the fact that it is so. Here is the Church's declaration that conviction of sin is the first stage in the work of conversion. Then follows the cry for mercy, and only after that, the blessed assurance of peace.

Marriage is fundamentally a civil contract; but while the Church fulfils in her office of holy matrimony all that the civil authority requires, she makes it quite plain that marriage in the Christian sense cannot be dissolved until death depart the contracting parties. She demands, moreover, that when her children enter into the marriage contract, they shall devoutly offer their union before the altar in presence of the faithful, as a most excellent sacrament or mystery of the spiritual marriage and unity between Christ and His Church. Thus Christ is invoked as a guest at the marriage ceremony, to beautify and adorn the honourable estate of matrimony, as he did by his first miracle in Cana of Galilee. Surely if the Prayer Book were taken as our guide, there would not be the unhappy restlessness in married life, which alas is now so common to the scandal of our English name.

Oh how wise is Holy Church in her counsels upon holy marriage—in the reasons that she gives why matrimony was ordained. She propounds three reasons in ascending order of dignity. In the lowest place she names the procreation of children; but if that were all, then the children would count for more than the wife, and the sacred dignity of Christian marriage would be lost. Next she names the remedy against sin; but if this were all, then marriage would be the refuge of the weak man rather than the vocation of the strong man. She rises to higher ground when she declares that Holy Matrimony was ordained "for the mutual society, help, and comfort, that the one ought to have of the other, both in prosperity and adversity."

Sooner or later all must expect sickness. And in this experience Holy Church is again at hand. "Whatsoever thy sickness is, be assured that it is God's visitation." The sick man's room is treated as a consecrated place, where Christ is suffering in the person of one of His members. The sick man's room is the only place outside the church, in which the priest has authority to celebrate the Holy Sacrament. And the Church of England shows the tenderest compassion for her suffering ones in being not content that the material sacrament should be carried from the church and baldly given to the sick man: rather she would dispense with rules which otherwise limit the action of the priest, that the Eucharistic offering itself may be made in the sick man's presence, that there be no sundering of the two things which Christ hath joined together, the pleading of the one sacrifice and the feeding thereupon.

And when the extreme hour of death arrives, the Church hath still her ministry of commendation, "We humbly commend the soul of this thy servant, our dear brother, into thy hands, as into the hands of a faithful Creator and most merciful Saviour, most humbly beseeching thee that it may be precious in thy sight."

But the Prayer Book gives no encouragement to the thought that opportunities of grace and probation here may be disregarded, and all the issues of this life be tried afresh hereafter. No special warrant is needed to authorize us to pray concerning those who have fallen asleep in Jesus, that they should advance from grace to grace in the nearer presence of their Lord. But no prayer of ours can avail to reverse the sentence of the particular judgment, or to bring Dives from across the gulf to the sweet peace of Abraham's bosom. Therefore, the Funeral Service in the Prayer Book is not an office of intercession for the departed, but an office of comfort and hope for the bereaved, an office of monition for all who remain. "Suffer us not at our last hour for any pains of death to fall from Thee."

Thus is the Book of Common Prayer our rule from birth to death, our guide in worship, and in our walk with God.

We can hardly exaggerate the good effect it has had in cherishing a sound and manly religion in England; neither on the one hand a religion of mere sentiment, finding its assurance in some debatable emotions, nor on the other hand a religion of mere ordinances, basing its hope, *ex opere operato*, on the performance of some mystic rites. We cannot be too thankful for the tone which the Prayer Book has given to worship in the English Church, wherein the spirits of the prophets are subject to the prophets, so that we are neither distracted in our worship by the ravings of an undisciplined faith, nor pained by expressions of familiarity unbecoming the approach of the creature to the Creator,—of the sinner to the Saviour; but wherein we are given an intelligent participation altogether distinct from that of spectators in a drama, or mere assistants in the performance of a mystery.

Thank God that we have a book so helpful, so instructive, so edifying, so apostolical, so evangelical, so catholic; a book incomparable in the literature of Christendom, a book worthy of its title as the book of COMMON PRAYER. God only give us grace to use it aright, and to live according to its standard.

XI.

THE LORD'S DAY.

"I was in the Spirit on the Lord's Day."—*Rev.* i. 10.

I SUBMIT to you this morning some practical considerations upon the observance of Sunday.

Some critics have doubted whether St John is here speaking of the weekly festival of the Christian Church. Some have argued that by "the Lord's Day" the apostle means Easter Day: others have strangely thought that he is referring to the Jewish, sabbath which God speaks of in the Old Testament as his holy day.

But we gather from contemporary writers that the term which the apostle uses, *the Dominical Day*, was in common use among Christians certainly in the second, and probably in the first century, as the appellation of the day which was otherwise known as *Dies Solis* or Sunday.

If anything was wanted, finally to close the

controversy, it was supplied by the discovery a few years ago of the treatise called "The Teaching of the Twelve Apostles." In this treatise we have directions for the Breaking of the Bread on every Lord's Day, and there is reason to conclude that the document is nearly as old as the book of the Revelation of St John. Some critics assign to it even an earlier date. But this is plain, that at the time of its composition the phrase "Dominical Day" had become such a technical term, such a mere name for the first day of the week, that its proper meaning was scarcely felt. People could speak of the Dominical Day without thinking of the Lord, just as we can speak of Sunday without thinking of the sun. This is clearly shown when the writer actually adds the explanatory words "of the Lord." He speaks of "the Dominical Day of the Lord," that is, "the Lord's day of the Lord." It is obvious that such a tautology would have been quite impossible unless "Dominical Day" or "Lord's Day" had become only a proper name. And there is no reasonable doubt that, in the text before us, St John is using the term in what seems to have already become its ordinary meaning when he says, "I was in the spirit on the Dominical Day."

o

Our Lord rose from the dead on the first day of the week, and he appeared to the assembled Church, and gave commission to his apostles on the evening of the same day. His next recorded appearance to them was on the following Sunday, and it was again on a Sunday, six weeks later, that He endowed his Church with the gifts of the Holy Ghost.

But the references to the observance of Sunday are few and far between in the New Testament. They are, however, of that incidental character which implies the reference to a well known and established custom. The historian of the Acts, describing St Paul's sojourn at Troas, speaks of "the first day of the week, when we came together to break bread." He gives no reason why they should have come together on this particular day, clearly assuming that the observance of the day is familiar to his readers. In like manner St Paul, writing to the Corinthians about the weekly offertory, mentions the first day of the week as the day on which their offerings should be made, and gives no reason for the arrangement, which he assumes to be in complete harmony with the custom of those to whom he writes.

It is quite clear, then, that Sunday was kept as

the Dominical Day in apostolic times. If we could determine *how* it was kept it would be easy to deduce some conclusions as to how it should be kept now.

Many have imagined that the Sunday was kept as the Jewish Sabbath. Some have even assumed that the apostles by some formal act transferred to the first day of the week the obligation which under the Mosaic law attached to the seventh day. There is no trace of any such transfer. On the contrary, there are clear indications that the Jewish Christians continued to keep the Jewish Sabbath long after they had begun to observe the Christian Lord's Day.

Some seventeen or eighteen years after the Resurrection a great question was discussed at the meeting of the Apostles at Jerusalem: it was admitted that *Jewish* Christians must observe the Mosaic law (including such ordinances as the Sabbath): but the question was whether *Gentiles* were forced to conform to Judaism on becoming Christians. Certain men came down from Judea and taught, saying, " Except ye be circumcised and keep the law [of Moses] ye cannot be saved." And some fifteen years later, St Paul, in writing to the Colossians, found it necessary to insist with some vehemence upon the truth that under the conditions of Christian liberty the obligation of the seventh day was not binding. This liberty was thus gradually established; but for the greater part of the first three decades after the Resurrection the Christians of Judea, and other Christians of Jewish origin, kept their Sabbath on Saturday, and celebrated the Resurrection every Sunday.

Did they, therefore, keep two sabbaths every week? Certainly not. Their observance of Sunday was something totally different from their observance of Saturday. Cessation from labour was the rule of Saturday: it was far from being the rule of Sunday.

When, however, the Church became more Gentile in its character, and when the destruction of Jerusalem witnessed to the End of the Jewish Dispensation, the distinction between Jew and Gentile in the Church was speedily obliterated, and the observance of the Sabbath passed away. But the underlying principle and spirit of the fourth commandment remained; the great principle that time is to be set apart for God in the devout performance of religious duties. And in carrying out this great principle it is likely enough that

Jewish Christians continued on Sunday some of the practices which they had been accustomed to associate with the Sabbath: in particular we may well believe that the Christian assemblies for reading and prayer on the Lord's Day were organized on the model of those Sabbath meetings in the Synagogue, in which our Lord himself had taken part. The Jewish habit of keeping Sabbath had thus a marked influence and effect in determining the character of the observance of the Lord's Day; and as the obligation of the Saturday-rest declined, the obligation of the Sunday observance seems to have been the more strongly enforced in the Church. But this is the utmost that can be said in support of the idea that in some sense the observance of the Sabbath was "transferred" by the Church to the first day of the week.

Nevertheless, from primitive days to the present, the keeping of Sunday has always been regarded as a duty of divine obligation, and the fourth commandment has always been appealed to in support of the practice. So the Church still reads the decalogue; and though there be no warrant for the assumption that the law of the Jewish Sabbath is of force to regulate the Christian Lord's Day, we must not rush to the opposite extreme and declare the Fourth Commandment to be obsolete. The fourth commandment in principle and spirit (as I have already defined it) is for all time.

The Jew was bound to separate and consecrate from all common use a tenth of his income and a seventh of his time. Perhaps in neither case is the precise rule of proportion binding on us. But we are bound to honour the Lord with our substance and to make oblation to his service of the fleeting hours. And it would be difficult to give a reason why the measure of Christian devotion (either as regards money or time) should come short of the measure of Jewish obligation. Certainly we cannot be said to be making a reasonable oblation of time to God if we devote half an hour in the morning to the Divine Service, and claim the rest of the day for our own pleasure. The continental Sunday may have a charm for some who find a special fascination in all that is continental in Ecclesiastical practices, but I know that devout clergy of the Roman Communion in France bitterly deplore the secularization of the Lord's Day by the State, and envy us our English Sunday. Moreover, we who are strong must bear the infirmities of the weak, and not please ourselves. We must see to it that our liberty become not a stumbling-block to others. We must consider the effect upon the community at large, of practices which we may deem innocent in the limited measure in which we adopt them, but which in excess are certainly sinful. "All things are lawful for me," says St Paul, "but all things are not expedient. All things are lawful for me, but all things edify not."

For example, men may say that they are only using their lawful liberty in Christ if they play cricket or football on Sunday afternoon. But it is very certain that if those whose example is respected in the community allow themselves this liberty, Sunday will soon become *the* day, the day of days, for sport; and we shall have not only our Sunday cricket matches, but our Sunday horse races! Will this edify? Will it further the cause of true religion? Will it build up the Church of Christ?

And here the question arises, "Are we bound to respect custom and convention in framing rules for our own observance of Sunday?"

I answer that unless we adopt in one extreme such a rule as that of the Jewish Sabbath, or in the other, such a rule as that of the continental

Sunday, our rule must necessarily involve much that is arbitrary and conventional. It is impossible by strict logic to draw a line and say thus far must I go and no farther in my reverence for the Lord's Day; the wise casuist must have regard to the conventions of the Church, and must even take account of the arbitrary conventions of the world. The strict logician may argue, "If I may talk of the news of the day, I may read the newspaper; if I may read the newspaper I may read in it the report of the stock market; if I may read the report of the stock market, I may determine what purchases to make to-morrow; if I may settle what purchases to make, I may write to my stock-broker and instruct him accordingly." But the devout Christian binds himself by conventional limitations on St Paul's principle that all things lawful are not convenient. One man therefore will not look at a newspaper on Sunday. Another will not write a letter. Another only restrains himself from letters of business. In other matters rules equally conventional may be made: not to read novels on Sunday, not to play games, not to take cabs, not to travel by public conveyances, not to travel except compelled by duty or charity, not to dine out, not to make calls, not to receive guests, not to do needlework, not to do gardening, and so on. Different rules will suit different persons, and each must be fully persuaded in his own mind.[1] But such distinctions as I have indicated, are so conventional, that we can conceive persons under different circumstances adopting even opposite rules. It may be very fitting for one person to devote a large part of Sunday to self-improvement and study, whilst for another person, differently situated, it may be a proper rule not to study on Sunday. But I would

---

[1] Some clergy do not scruple to travel by omnibus or rail in order to take duty on Sunday, though they would not travel for mere pleasure. Others refuse to go out to preach, unless the church can be reached on foot or on cycle. Cycling appears to be less open to objection than any other artificial means of locomotion, because it imposes no labour upon any but the traveller himself, and in many country parishes the clergy are thus enabled to reach outlying mission chapels which otherwise they would not be able to serve. Yet the world in London is slow to surrender the prejudice that cycling is a mere pastime or amusement. On a recent Sunday evening I was engaged to preach in a suburban church at a distance of five miles. If I had employed the labour of others, travelling by cab or omnibus, none probably would have raised any objection; but as I rode my cycle, I was saluted by street loiterers with the question, "Is that what they teach in Church?"

have you note two points: (1) That however conventional a rule may be, it may be valuable if it only serve to mark a difference between Sundays and other days; and (2) that if our observance of Sunday is to be a witness to the world, we must give due consideration to the prejudices and conventions of the world.

My brethren, there is no religion of Christ without the bearing of the Cross of self-denial. Now if you look at the masses of Christian people in this country, you will perceive that there is only one form of religious self-denial known to the great majority of them. There may be much moral self-denial amongst them— a thing of beauty and of glory in their lives, the self-denial of kindness and of an enthusiasm of humanity: a self-denial in the faithful and large-hearted discharge of duty. But in religion—Do they fast? No. Do they perform some penance when they have sinned? No. These traditions have been lost amongst them. But they do one thing—they keep Sunday. And this Sunday-keeping has been the salt of self-denial which has preserved the religion of England from rottenness, whilst so much of the Protestantism of Europe has become the empty and effete thing which we know it to be. Sunday-keeping is the one exercise of religious self-denial for the majority of our countrymen. I beseech you, do nothing to rob them of it.

And let it never be forgotten that the keeping of Sunday is of far higher obligation than the observance of any other festival or Solemn Day. The Lord's Day stands on higher ground than even Christmas Day, or Good Friday, or Ascension Day. These belong to a later age of the Church, but the appropriation of Sunday as the special day on which Christians should meet together for worship received the sanction of our Lord Himself by his appearance to the assembled Church on the Resurrection Day, and on its octave; it was consecrated by the giving of the Holy Ghost on Whit-sunday: and we have the witness of the apostles and the primitive Church to the continuity of the observance.

Surely it betrays a want of the sense of proportion when a Saint's Day, which is not a Sunday, seems sometimes to be preferred in honour above a Sunday which is not a Saint's Day.

There is no weekday in the year which appeals so strongly to our religious feeling as Good Friday. But the obligation to observe Good

Friday is certainly less than the obligation to keep Sunday. I doubt the wisdom of pressing the strict observance of Good Friday as a positive duty upon any except the more devout; and the really devout will keep the day, not so much of obligation as of devotion. The Three Hours' Meditations were originally introduced for the benefit of those who had reached some depth of spiritual life. But now it has become established, almost as a canon of propriety, that the most careless churchman must be present at least for some portion of the meditations. And in many quarters it is deemed a greater sin to make Good Friday a holiday than to desecrate Sunday.

It was not always so. The Church has ever felt that the observance of Sunday was binding upon all; but she has been disposed to establish other holy days as spiritual opportunities for those of habitual leisure, but as times of relaxation for those who were engaged in continuous labour. In my boyhood, in the village where my father was parish priest, the afternoon of Good Friday was always devoted by the labourers to the cultivation of their own gardens; and I venture to say that this was entirely in accordance with the mind of the Church of olden days. It was the ancient custom that the rich should lend their beasts to the poor for the tillage of their land on Good Friday, though on Sunday man and beast alike were to rest. And the Church, in her habitual care for the poor, sanctioned this custom. Thus we find Simon Mepham, who was Archbishop of Canterbury from 1328 to 1333, issuing a constitution for the observance of Good Friday, but carefully guarding the privileges of the poor. Thus he writes:

We strictly prohibit that in future anyone should occupy himself with servile work on that day, or should do anything else which is inconsistent with devout celebration. Nevertheless, we do not by this law mean to lay a burden upon the poor, nor put any obstacle in the way of the rich to prevent their affording the customary assistance for charity's sake to help on the tillage of their poorer neighbours.[1]

But if I may give you a rule for the intelligent observance of the Lord's Day, let it be this: that you think of what you must do, rather than of what you must not do. Is it not the characteristic contrast of the law and the gospel

---

[1] Quoted by Father Thurston, S.J., in the "Nineteenth Century," July, 1899.

that Moses said *Thou shalt not*, and Christ said *Thou shalt?*

Moses said, "Thou shalt not have other gods, thou shalt not make a graven image, thou shalt not take God's name in vain, thou shalt not do any work on the Sabbath." But Christ fulfils it all in the positive command, "Thou shalt love the Lord thy God with all thy heart." So Moses forbad murder, adultery, theft, slander, and covetousness. But Christ included all these in the precept, "Thou shalt love thy neighbour as thyself." The Jew was guarded on the right hand and on the left by prohibitions, but the child of God in Jesus Christ is taught that love is the fulfilling of the law.

And it is interesting to notice that the rules which the Church of England gives her faithful sons for the observance of Sunday are positive in their character. She does not furnish us with a list of things which we must not do, but she sets before us clearly the objects of the Lord's Day, expounding the good purposes for which the day is to be used. We read the mind of the Church in the 13th Canon of 1603, which runs as follows:

All manner of persons within the Church of England shall from henceforth celebrate and keep the

Lord's Day, commonly called Sunday, according to God's holy will and pleasure, and the orders of the Church of England prescribed in that behalf; that is, in hearing the Word of God read and taught; in private and public prayers; in acknowledging their offences to God and amendment of the same; in reconciling themselves charitably to their neighbours where displeasure hath been; in oftentimes receiving the communion of the body and blood of Christ; in visiting of the poor and sick; using all godly and sober conversation.

What a beautiful and blessed day is here described! a day given up to prayer and praise, to the seeking of spiritual instruction, to the deepening of the spiritual life, to works of charity in the largest sense of the term. How different is such a day from a mere Sabbath of cessation from labour and abstinence from the pleasures of the world. The day of mere rest may be a day of uselessness, a day wasted, a day lost; but the holy day which the Church calls her children to keep is fraught with high purposes and holy business, a day of blessing to the man who keeps it aright, a day of blessing also to those who are objects of his holy charity.

Though the canon says nothing of cessation from work, the Church doubtless takes it for granted that this will be. But the work is not to be put aside as if the mere cessation from it were an end in itself. It is to be put aside in order that there may be room for those spiritual occupations which the canon enumerates.

And amongst these, note first that the Church expects the Sunday to afford time for private devotion as well as for public worship. Her faithful children are to celebrate and keep the Lord's Day "in private and public prayers," and the intention evidently is that opportunity shall be found for something more than the private prayers of every day. The careful Bible study, the reading of books of spiritual instruction, the acts of praise, the meditations which have perhaps been crowded out of the busy life of the week, may well occupy us in the spiritual retirement of Sunday.

Note, secondly, that anything which belongs to our conflict with sin, anything in fact which is to make us better, is a proper occupation for Sunday. The day is to be kept "in acknowledging our offences to God, and in amendment of the same." If we kept this purpose in view, surely the Sunday would not be the vain and empty day that it too often appears to be.

Note, also, that the charitable work of Sunday is to begin with that Divine charity that seeks peace on earth in the reconciliation of those who are estranged. The faithful are to keep the day "in reconciling themselves charitably to their neighbours where displeasure hath been." Go and be an angel of peace among your brethren. Such angel's work is Sunday work indeed.

But works of charity in regard to the bodily life are not to be overlooked. You observe that the day is to be kept "in visiting of the poor and sick." This, perhaps, is not commonly counted among Sunday duties. How many of us, for example, examining ourselves as to the way in which we have spent a Sunday, would think of asking of our conscience the question, Have I visited the poor and sick? I do not say that the rule is to be literally and narrowly pressed. It may be largely interpreted to include many analogous duties. To gather some poor children together, to teach them, may be much the same thing as to visit them in their homes, and may fulfil the intention of the Church. But at least it should be remembered that the Church enumerates the visiting of the poor and sick amongst the ordinary occupations of a good man's Sunday.

It is, perhaps, because such occupations are neglected that it sometimes seems so hard to fill up the hours of the Lord's Day appropriately. We cannot be always in church : we cannot read the Bible all the day. How often is this made the ground of an excuse for some frivolous occupation? But has the Church's bidding been done, in some spiritual and equivalent sense, in visiting of the poor and sick?

But the climax of the Church's rule is found in the injunction that Sundays and Holy-days are to be kept "in oftentimes receiving the communion of the body and blood of Christ." There is not the slightest indication that any obligation is discharged by mere presence at the service. The state of Christian privilege is marked by the " oftentimes receiving." And it was thus that the first day of the week was kept from the beginning. The same adjective was applied to the day itself and to the feast (either to the Eucharist itself or to the feast of charity which accompanied the Eucharist). The one was the Dominical Day, the other the Dominical Supper. And the adjective is used in no other connection in the New Testament. The Lord's Feast is the only recognized keeping of the Lord's Day.

My brethren, I commend to you the rule of our Mother Church in this matter: the rule which is in harmony with apostolic and primitive practice: the rule which is wiser and better than any rule of private judgment, and comes to us with an authority which no rule of our own devising can possess; the rule that is Christian rather than Mosaic; a rule positive rather than negative; a rule of counsels rather than of prohibitions. Take it, as in duty bound, to be the guide to your Sunday observance. So shall you be enabled at the last to look back with thankfulness on the Sundays of your Christian life, and to say concerning them, " I was in the Spirit on the Lord's Day."

XII.

THE DOCTRINE OF CHRISTIAN WORSHIP.

"Your reasonable service."—*Rom.* xii. 1.

OUR subject is the doctrine of Christian worship.

Neither you nor I should be willing to devote this sacred hour to the consideration of mere ceremonial. But in recent controversies the importance of ceremonial has been accentuated in two respects:

I. Our ceremonial usage is a witness to the regard which we have for the authority of the Church.

II. It is an expression of our faith as to the conditions of our approach to God under the covenant of Christian worship.

I. The first point need scarcely detain us. We show our belief in the English Church as a living branch of the Church Universal by obedience to her rule. If the Church of England in

1661 was no true church, then the Prayer Book has no spiritual authority. Conversely, if the Prayer Book, which was delivered to us with every sanction which the Church as a spiritual body could give, be without authority, it can only be so because the Church was impotent and her living voice was void. The validity of the Prayer Book stands or falls with the validity of our Church's claim to be a living and true branch of the Catholic Church. We may refer to Catholic antiquity to interpret the Prayer Book, but as soon as we set up Catholic precedent (or our private judgment of it) to supersede or correct the Prayer Book, we are making ourselves to be wiser than our Church, and are implicitly denying her spiritual authority. That be far from us! Here the Prayer Book is the acknowledged standard. We can neither symbolize with those, on the one hand, who have studied the liturgy to so little purpose that they can habitually, but "unintentionally," omit from the Communion Service the scriptural lessons, the epistle and gospel, which from the earliest ages have formed part of the rite, nor with those, on the other hand, who desire (as they say) to enrich our Communion Service, either by the restoration of phrases which the Church in her spiritual wisdom rejected, or by the introduction of modern features from foreign rites.

I have said enough on this point. Let us rather give our attention to the doctrine of worship, as it is expressed by the ceremonial of the Church.

II. The present controversies as to ceremonial are substantially controversies as to the doctrine of Christian worship, especially in regard to that intensest form of Christian worship which is offered in Holy Communion.

On this subject there appears to exist much confusion of thought, even amongst churchmen who suppose that they hold the Catholic doctrine of the Real Presence.

I do not think it would be profitable for us to discuss the views of those who deny the sacrificial aspect of the Holy Eucharist; who deny that we are pleading the one sacrifice of the Cross in retrospect, as truly as the Jews of old in their sacrifices pleaded it in prospect; who assert that the showing of the Lord's death till He come, means that we show it one to another; who deny that we present it to God, putting Him in remembrance thereof, and thus making the Lord's death our plea; who declare that the whole benefit of Communion is subjective, that if it cause us to think of Christ as the Saviour, and encourage us to meditate upon the supreme efficacy of his death, it has done all that it can do for us, and everything that it was ordained to do.

I leave these views aside. I am speaking to those who believe that our Lord is present in the Holy Eucharist, in some sense in which He cannot be said to be present at our other services. But amongst those who hold this position there is a serious divergence of opinion as to what this real presence implies, a divergence of opinion which necessarily leads to a very great diversity of practice in Christian worship.

Many arguments which are commonly propounded on the subject of Eucharistic worship, fall to the ground at once when it is remembered that the question is not what is there present in the Holy Eucharist?—but what is there present in the Holy Eucharist *which is absent at other times?* It is not: In what sense is Christ present in Holy Communion? but, In what sense is He present in Holy Communion *exclusively?* that is, In what sense is He absent at mattins and evensong, but present when the Holy Sacrament is on the altar? It is, therefore, perfectly futile to suppose that all difficulties are disposed of at once by the syllogism:

Where Christ is present there He is to be worshipped.
Christ is present in the Blessed Sacrament.
Therefore He is to be worshipped in the Blessed Sacrament.

For we are immediately confronted by another syllogism:

Where Christ is present there He is to be worshipped.
Christ is present everywhere.
Therefore He is to be worshipped everywhere.

A distinction may indeed be drawn in the terms of a catechism, issued by a society of English clergy, wherein we find the question and answer:

Q. Where is our Lord Jesus Christ?
A. Our Lord Jesus Christ as God is everywhere; as God and Man He is in heaven and in the Blessed Sacrament of the altar.

But this distinction will not help those who maintain that the Sacramental Presence con-

The Doctrine of Christian Worship.

stitutes a special object of worship, for it is an axiom of the Christian Faith that worship is to be addressed to Christ as God. We may claim his intercession as God and man, but the Sacred Humanity can add nothing to the Divinity as an object of that worship which is due to God only.

All are agreed that Christ is to be worshipped in the Blessed Sacrament, as He is to be worshipped wherever He is present. All are agreed also that the receiving of Holy Communion is an act of worship which is impossible where the Sacrament is not. But we ask, what authority is there for the allegation that (apart from Communion) our Lord is to be worshipped in the Blessed Sacrament, more or more acceptably than wherever else two or three are gathered together in his Name, and He is there in the midst of them? This question can only be answered by reference to our Lord's institution; for the second commandment is in its spirit for all time the rule of worship; and its spiritual import is this, that we must worship God, not according to man's device, but in the way of God's appointment.

For myself, when I am asked for a definition

of the Presence of Christ in the Eucharist, distinguishing that presence from his presence at other times where two or three are gathered together in his Name, I am content to say that Christ is present in the Holy Eucharist in the mode in which He is pleased to impart Himself to us for the strengthening and refreshing of our souls, and under the conditions which admit of our performance of the most intense action of Christian worship. Or (which is the same thing) we may say that Christ is present in the Sacrament in the mode in which He is pleased to give us to eat his flesh and to drink his blood, that we may show his Death till He come.

At other times He may be present in the mode in which He is to be worshipped, as at mattins, at evensong, in the prayer meeting, in family prayer, in the innermost chamber of private devotion; but on these occasions He is not present in the mode in which He is pleased to give us his flesh to eat, his blood to drink, nor have we opportunity of offering the most sacred pledge of our allegiance to Him.

On these definitions, as far as they go, we shall all be agreed. But you will observe that they concern the communicant alone. If the Sacrament is of any concern to the person who is not receiving it, some further explanation is necessary. Is it then true to say that for those who are not receiving the Sacrament there is in the Sacrament an object of worship which is absent at other times? Is it true to say that Christ is present then, and not at other times, in the mode in which our worship is most acceptable?

Now it must be admitted that if the Real Presence constitutes an object of worship which is absent when the Sacrament is not before us, we ought to have the Sacrament reserved at all times in our churches. Or if our worship is more acceptable to our Lord when offered before the Sacrament, why should we ever be without the Sacrament? On such an hypothesis, the Church that gave up Reservation would be placing her devout children at an intolerable disadvantage, and would be defrauding our Lord of his due honour. On such an hypothesis, to make Reservation dependent upon the accident of the Sacrament being required for the sick would be an outrage upon the glory of the Lord—making his honour in his Church to be contingent upon the need or convenience of his servants. On such an hypothesis, the Church of England is altogether out of court, and her position indefensible. Her doom is in that case sealed; for who could remain in allegiance to a Church that robbed Christ of his glory and man of his appointed means of access to God?

But what ground is there for the supposition that the Sacrament on the altar constitutes an object of worship which is absent at other times, or that the presence of Christ in the mode in which He gives us his flesh to eat and his blood to drink, accords a special efficacy to the prayers of those who are *not* eating his flesh and drinking his blood? There is certainly no ground whatever in Holy Scripture; and it is very dangerous to say that one mode of worship is more acceptable to God than another, unless we have divine warrant for the distinction. Moreover, the precedents which have been cited from the practice of the early Church in favour of Reservation are altogether adverse to the idea that the Sacrament should be reserved for worship. It is quite certain that early in the second century all the faithful who could be present communicated every Lord's Day, and the Sacrament was taken away to those who by sickness or any other cause were hindered from attending: but there is not a hint of the reservation for the purpose of worship. Later in the same century portions of the Sacrament were carried away and kept in caskets or worn about the person as a charm, until the Church found it necessary to enact canons to restrain this superstitious misuse of that which had been ordained for a different purpose. But the very fact that for many years such an abuse was allowed is incompatible with the hypothesis that the consecrated elements were thought of as constituting a new object of worship. The very fact that a devout woman could keep the Sacrament in her house and partake of it in family life before all food points not to an exaggerated idea of the Real Presence, but the reverse.

But, sirs, neither you nor I accept the hypothesis of which we speak. We do not believe that the Christ whom we worship has been absent from the service in which we have been joining.[1] He has been absent, indeed, in the mode in which He gives us his flesh to eat and his blood to drink. We shall in the next hour call Him to be present in that most sacred mode.

---

[1] This sermon was preached at the conclusion of Mattins, when a celebration of the Holy Eucharist was to follow.

But during mattins He has not been absent in the mode in which He is pleased that we should draw near to the Father through Him, nor absent in the mode in which his own Very Deity is the object of our worship. We do not believe that the promise, "Where two or three are gathered together in my Name there am I in the midst," is fulfilled *only* when the Sacrament is on the altar. We do not believe that the worship in which we have been engaged would have been more acceptable to Him, or that the prayers which we have offered would have been more efficacious, if in the sanctuary yonder there had been a tabernacle in which the Blessed Sacrament were reserved. We do not believe that the celebration of Holy Communion which presently follows—unless we are going therein to eat the flesh of the son of man and drink his blood—will constitute for us a higher act of worship or a more acceptable approach to God, or an action of greater honour to our Lord, or an occasion of more efficacious prayer, than that in which we have already joined.

Ought we, then, to discourage the presence at the holy mysteries of those who are not receiving the Holy Sacrament? Certainly not, provided that they are coming in a right spirit, and with no superstitious intention. It is true that the Church in the early ages forbad the presence of those who were not receiving, but at a later epoch this rule was relaxed. We may accept the liberty which the Church of later ages accorded to her children, the more so as there is a special significance, a testimony of faith and devotion in attendance at the celebration, even without communion.

But if we found people attending the celebration with the idea that they would find therein an object of worship absent from the other services, then we should act in the spirit of Hezekiah who destroyed the Brazen Serpent which Moses had made, and called it Nehustan—because the children of Israel had begun to burn incense to it. For to find in the consecrated elements an object of worship which is absent elsewhere is the grossest violation of the second commandment. It is the worshipping of God not in the way that he has ordained, but in a way of man's devising. If we thought that our people could be guilty of such idolatry it would be our duty to discourage by all legal means their presence as non-communicants at the celebration of the mysteries.

There is, however (as we have said), the right spirit and the right intention with which the faithful may participate in the worship which we offer in the Eucharist, though they be not at the time partakers of the sacrificial feast. And they must be encouraged to come with a special devotion which is not drawn out in the same way in any other service. It is not devotion to an object otherwise absent, but it is devotion to that aspect of our Lord's work which the Blessed Sacrament expresses, it is devotion to our Lord as giving Himself for the life of the world, imparting Himself to us, making his body to be the bread of life, and his blood the saving of our souls.

And here we may note the reason of that distinction of personal ritual which is customary in presence of the Blessed Sacrament. Again I say it does not imply that there is something now to be adored which at other times is absent, but the faithful bow the knee in deeper reverence in devotion to that great love of Christ of which the Sacrament is witness—just as at other times they bow at the name of the Lord Jesus in devout remembrance of the Incarnation.

The normal purpose of Christ's institution of the Blessed Sacrament is that men should receive it; and a system under which communion becomes the exception, and non-communicating attendance the rule, is a manifest violation of our Lord's intention, and of the practice of the primitive Church. But if you habitually receive the Blessed Sacrament, and yet desire to be present on some occasion on which you do not receive it, the Church of the later centuries allows it, and you may make it an act of the sweetest devotion. Only remember what it means: it must be a witness to the deep devotion of your heart to all that the Blessed Sacrament expresses.

But it is difficult to understand how one who habitually neglects Communion, can profess any particular devotion to the Sacrament or to that aspect of our Lord's work for us which the Blessed Sacrament presents. If a man is unfit for Communion because he will not take the trouble to prepare for it—because he shrinks from self-examination and penitence—because he counts the surrender of sin a greater sacrifice than he is willing to make,—and yet ventures to kneel among the faithful at the celebration of the Eucharist, professing amongst God's people a reverence and devotion for the Sacrament which he uses not,—surely such an one feedeth on ashes: a deceived heart hath turned him aside that he cannot deliver his soul nor say, "Is there not a lie in my right hand?"

There is one mistake upon this subject which I find to be widely prevalent. It is supposed that the Church enjoins her children to be present at the Holy Eucharist on every Sunday and holy day, whether they communicate or not. The Church of England knows no such rule. Non-communicating attendance may be permitted, but it is nowhere enjoined. The Church of England in the Prayer Book calls her lay people as well as her clergy to the Divine Office of mattins and evensong, and she exhorts them to frequent and regular Communion.

The Roman Church instructs her faithful to hear mass on Sundays and holy days of obligation; and this rule probably prevailed in the unreformed Church of England. There was, in fact, no other public service in which the laity could discharge the obligation of public worship in the church. But it was, I think, one of the happiest changes made at the Reformation that the Divine Office of the Hours was translated into a form convenient for laity as well as clergy, and the priest was directed to ring a bell before

The Doctrine of Christian Worship.

his daily mattins and evensong, that the people might come and hear God's word and pray with him. There is the mind of the Church of England plainly set forth as to the services in which she calls you to join.

And I need not remind you how urgent is her call to Communion. "Consider," she says, "how great injury ye do unto God, and how sore punishment hangeth over your heads for neglect, when ye wilfully abstain from the Lord's table and separate from your brethren who come to feed on the banquet of that most heavenly food." You remember how she bids the minister plead with the people: "According to mine office I bid you in the name of God, I call you on Christ's behalf, I exhort you as ye love your own salvation, that ye will be partakers of this Holy Communion."

The doctrine of Christian worship is therefore briefly this: we worship God whether we address our prayers to the Person of the Father in the name of the Son, or whether we address them to the Person of the Son in that divinity in which He is with the Father and the Holy Ghost one God omniscient and omnipresent. The object of our worship cannot be localized in the Eucharistic elements nor limited by any conditions of space. In the mode in which He gives Himself to feed our souls, our Lord is present in the Holy Eucharist and absent elsewhere. But in the mode in which He presents Himself as the object of our worship, He is never absent from the assembly of the faithful. But though He is always present, and cannot be more or less present as the object of our worship, our worship may be more or less acceptable before his throne according to the degree in which it corresponds to his intention and to the terms of his covenant of prayer. Our highest act of worship is, therefore, that which He Himself instituted, that pledge of devout allegiance to his service which we take when we receive the Blessed Sacrament of his Body and Blood. In the Holy Eucharist the Church offers the most solemn act of worship, and as devout worshippers we join individually in the offering; but as Christ has ordained the way by which we are to participate in the Holy Eucharist (viz., by receiving the Blessed Sacrament), we cannot be said to join in the Eucharistic worship in any other way. The man who thinks to join in the Eucharistic sacrifice without receiving the Sacrament, is precisely in the same position as the man who claims to be a member of the Church because he believes in Christ, without being baptized. Baptism is the appointed way by which we become members of the mystical body of Christ, and the receiving of Holy Communion is the appointed way by which we participate in the Eucharistic oblation. But our presence at a baptism may be an act of devout remembrance of our membership in Christ, and our presence at the Holy Eucharist may be an act of intense devotion to the atoning work of Christ which is therein signified. But as it is, after all, an act only of private judgment and personal devotion, let us be careful first to fulfil the behests of the Church, who calls us to the daily offices of prayer and praise, and to frequent Communion.

Worship is the spontaneous expression of faith, and without faith worship is impossible. Worship is an act of confession and submission: it is an act of obedience and self-surrender: it is an act of love and devotion: it is an act of reverence and godly fear: it is an act of thanksgiving and of praise.

Sometimes the worshipper is occupied with his own needs—he cries to God for help and deliverance, for gifts of life temporal or spiritual. But even his cry is the evidence of faith in the power of God to grant him the blessing that he craves; and his petition is always offered with the reservation of the divine will. He lays the wants before his God, but he adds, "Nevertheless, not as I will, but as Thou wilt."

Happier is he in his worship when he prays, not for himself, but for others, and pleads the Name of Christ for his fellow members in the Body of Christ, or for his brethren in the common humanity for which Christ died.

Happier, when he passes from petition to thanksgiving, recognizing the hand of God in the dispensations of providence and grace, and acknowledging the wisdom and the love of the heavenly Father therein.

Happiest of all, when his worship culminates in praise. Self and self-interest are forgotten. He is no longer thanking God for what He does, but he is praising God for what He is. He bows his head in awful reverence, and cries: "Holy: Holy: Holy: Lord God of Hosts: the fulness of the earth is thy glory."

But he worships not alone: he worships in the company of the saints, in the Body of Christ. His confession, his petition, his intercession, his thanksgiving, his praise, all are offered in the fellowship of the Church and in the Name of Jesus Christ; all are included in the Church's great action of worship, in the celebration of the Holy Eucharist.

But one last word. Our worship, however it be offered, is altogether vain unless it express the offering of ourselves. It must register the fact of our devotion in living sacrifice to God. "I beseech you, therefore, brethren, by the mercies of God, that ye present your bodies a living sacrifice, holy, acceptable unto God, which is your reasonable service."

NOTE

ON THE MIND OF THE CHURCH OF ENGLAND AS TO "HEARING MASS."

The following passages from an address delivered at Sion College are added here as further elucidating the position maintained in the sermon.

THESIS.—"That in the mind of the Church of England those who are not receiving Holy Communion on the Lord's Day, should rather 'assist at Mattins' than 'hear Mass.'"

There is no question as to the ideal of worship set before the devout Christian by Holy Church. The

Liturgy and the Divine Office are for him. He is called to both. He will receive his communion and, if it may be, he will join in Mattins and Evensong.

But the Church has to care for many who fall far short of the ideal. In primitive times all who were present at the celebration of Holy Communion invariably communicated, and the Sacrament was carried to those who were unavoidably absent. No one was thought to keep the Lord's Day except he partook of the Lord's Table.

But as the centuries advanced and love grew cold, many were found to claim a place in the fold of Christ, though they had not the devotion to fit them to receive the Sacrament Sunday by Sunday. The best thing that can be said for them is that they had faith to prevent them coming unworthily. As early as the fourth century we find Communion neglected, but those who did not receive went out with the Catechumens or else came not to the Celebration at all. They were condemned for such neglect of duty. Thus in the apostolic constitutions we find the enactment "all such of the faithful as come to Church and hear the Scriptures read, but stay not for the Prayers and to partake of the Holy Communion, ought to be suspended as authors of disorder in the Church." And St Chrysostom complains: "I often observe a great multitude flock together to hear the sermon, but when the time of the Holy Mysteries comes I can see few or none of them."

But a few centuries later we find another practice prevailing. Persons would come to the Celebration

The Doctrine of Christian Worship. 233

of the Holy Mysteries but draw not nigh to receive the Sacrament.

In the ninth century the Church strenuously endeavoured to put a stop to this, and published, among the forged decretals, what purported to be a decree of Anacletus, ordering all present to communicate on pain of excommunication. It was, however, found impossible to check a custom which accorded well with the laxity of the times, and at length the Church yielded to the exigency of the situation, and reluctantly sanctioned a practice which it was powerless to resist.

From this time Communion appears to have become rapidly rarer and more rare, until at length the receiving of the Body and Blood of Christ by the laity was altogether divorced from the Eucharistic service. St Paul had said: "As often as ye eat this Bread and drink this Cup ye do show the Lord's death till He come." But men thought that they could show the Lord's death without eating the Bread and drinking the Cup, by simple assistance at the service. It was enough, they thought, if once a year they made their confession and were privately Communicated with the reserved Sacrament. So the Sarum Missal, in use in England until the Reformation, makes no provision whatever for the Communion of the people.

The first care of the Reformers was to make the Communion of the people an integral part of the service, and so to re-unite the two actions of Worship and Communion which Christ had joined together but man had put asunder. To emphasize the more clearly the close connection between "Do this" and "Take, eat," the Church of England still ordains that there shall be no celebration unless there be three at the least to communicate with the priest.

And the Reformers seem to have fondly hoped at the first that all would be at least occasional communicants. For example, it was ordered in 1549 that at a wedding the bride and bridegroom the same day of their marriage *must* receive the Holy Communion, and not until 1661 was this softened by the phrase, "it is convenient."

But the Reformers were never so infatuated as to hope that all would become regular communicants. It was recognized in 1549 that many would communicate only once a year, a minimum qualification which was increased in 1552 to three times in a year.

What, then, was the intention of the Church—what is still the mind of the Church—with regard to those who, on any given Sunday, are not communicating?

If the Church intends that they should go out after the sermon with the unbaptized and excommunicate, she is certainly following Catholic precedent. For those who declare themselves unfit for Communion, are, in fact, at the tribunal of their own conscience, excommunicate. This is, in very truth, the form of excommunication on which our English Church relies. She does not hastily hale her children before an ecclesiastical judge, but she teaches them, in those valuable exhortations, which have no parallel in any other Liturgy, what is fitness for Communion, and what constitutes unfitness: and she calls them to judgment before the Holy Ghost in the tribunal of the heart.

It must, however, be admitted that the Church of England has never revoked the liberty accorded to the devout non-communicant in the ninth century of being present while the Holy Mysteries are celebrated. And it is quite clear that there is much in the Liturgy in which a devout churchman can join, though he be not on that particular occasion receiving the Sacrament or showing the Lord's death till He come. It may be admitted further that the associations connected with the most solemn rite of our Holy Religion may constitute a special help to devotion, to those who are joining in the service though not communicating. If this is what is meant by non-communicating attendance, not a word is to be said against it.

But something else is meant by those who assert that it is the duty of every churchman every Sunday to "hear Mass." (This is the technical phrase which connotes what I think is a totally erroneous view of the Eucharistic Sacrifice.)

I. I maintain that there is not the slightest warrant for the assertion that in default of Communion the Church expects, or calls, or advises her children to hear Mass. I have already quoted the rubric of the bell which secures for every churchman the privilege of joining in the Divine Office: but there is no similar rubric in regard to the Liturgy. A far-fetched argument is sometimes deduced from the direction that the baptized child is to hear sermons, and it is said that the only sermon ordered by the Church occurs in the Communion Service. But this argument falls to the ground in view of the Catholic custom continuously followed in the Church of England from the Reformation if not before, that the uninitiated should withdraw after the sermon.

II. I deny that in hearing Mass the faithful are, as is alleged, showing the Lord's death. In the early centuries those penitents who were admitted on sufferance as *consistentes* were told that they could neither communicate nor join in offering the Oblation, the two must go together. We cannot get behind St Paul's rule that we show the Lord's death by eating the Bread and drinking the Cup.

III. I deny that there is in the Holy Eucharist for non-communicants an object of worship which is not to be found in the other services of the Church. The object of worship is Christ as God. Not the Body and Blood of Christ, but the Eternal Son of God who is present with us always, under the conditions in which he is to be worshipped: but present in the Sacrament, in the mode in which he communicates Himself to the faithful, for the strengthening and refreshing, yea, for the very life of their souls.

Certainly the Reformers did not contemplate that a mixed congregation, some communicating and others not communicating, should be kneeling together. In 1548, when the priest had given the warning, "lest the devil enter into him as he did into Judas," he was to "pause awhile to see if any man will withdraw himself." In 1549 the communicants were to tarry in the choir, the others, if they did not leave the Church, retiring at least to the nave which, in those days, was treated in many respects as a public place of common resort.

On these grounds I submit to you the thesis that it is the mind of the Church of England that those who are not communicating on the Lord's Day should rather "assist at Mattins" than "hear Mass."

* * * * *

There never has been a time in the history of the Church when churchmen have joined in public worship so little as they do at present. Throughout the eighteenth century we were a worshipping people. When St Anne's, Soho, was first built, daily prayers were said at six a.m. and six p.m. But in a few years it was found necessary to double these services, and during the whole of the eighteenth century Mattins at six and ten, Evensong at four and six, appear to have been well attended. But a precedent for these four services had been afforded in the previous century by Bishop Patrick, who, as rector of St Paul's, Covent Garden, established double Mattins and Evensong daily in that church. In a letter of Bishop Beveridge it is casually remarked that many Londoners were as constant at their public devotions daily as in their private business. Sir Walter Besant tells us that in 1750 there were daily services in forty-four of the churches within the city limits. The volume entitled "Pietas Londinensis" ran through many editions. It was a guide to devout Londoners, showing them that at every hour of the day from early morning till evening the Divine Office was being said somewhere in London. The first literary effort of the late Upton Richards as a young man was to re-edit this volume; but by this time the practice of daily worship was falling away. Yet as late as the year 1815 a guide to Tunbridge Wells, describing the mode in which the fashionable company spent the day, says: "After breakfast it is customary to attend Morning Service in the chapel. . . . Prayers over, the music re-commences." How differently would a present-day description read! By the middle of the present century daily services had become quite exceptional. In 1848 a writer mentions the Temple Church, Westminster Abbey, St Mark's, Chelsea, Margaret Chapel, and Christ Church, Albany Street, as the churches known to him where this privilege could be found.

There is no doubt that this lamentable declension was largely due to the fact that under the evangelical revival public worship was judged not as an act of homage to God, but as a means of personal edification. And personal edification might be as well pursued in private.

But the Catholic Revival restored a truer conception, and we read of the peer of the realm and the literary man and the employée in the millinery establishment, travelling in an early morning in 1848 to begin their day with Mattins at Christ Church, Albany Street. The noble laymen who gave their strength to the Oxford Movement, showed in their daily practice their high conception of duty in regard to the Divine Office.

But now, alas, all is changed. The old Tractarians have been succeeded by a new generation in whose eyes Mattins and Evensong are of little account.

Happy, indeed, now as ever, are those who live in communion with God and fulfil the ideal of Christian Worship: who keep the Lord's Day by participation in the Lord's service; habitually pleading the virtue of the One Sacrifice, Oblation and Satisfaction for their sins; eating the flesh of the Son of Man and drinking his blood; showing the Lord's death till He come.

But alas for the multitudes who reach not this ideal. The Lord's Day comes round, and they are unready for communion. In their conscience they judge themselves unfit to take part in the offering of the great Oblation. Is there no lesser act of worship in which they may join, by which they may be led on and prepared for the greater? Are there no confessions and prayers in which they may unite with the Church? Is there nothing for them in the manifold experiences of the psalms? May they not be helped by lessons and by sermons? Alas for them! Grace only is to be found in hearing Mass! And if in their inward consciousness men feel that this strange and barren assistance at the Holy Mysteries is not for them, then there is nothing for them! Let them stay at home! The recital of the Psalter is obsolete! The Divine Office is of no account!

Thus are the most precious fruits of the Reformation ruthlessly cast away.